Life
Transformed

*Meditations on the Christian Scriptures
In Light of Buddhist Perspectives*

by *LEO LEFEBURE*

D0879259

ACTA PUBLICATIONS
CHICAGO, ILLINOIS

Life Transformed
Meditations on the Christian Scriptures in Light of Buddhist Perspectives
by Rev. Leo D. Lefebure, Ph.D.

Fr. Lefebure is assistant professor of systematic theology at Mundelein Seminary of the University of St. Mary of the Lake. He is a member of the Society for Buddhist-Christian Studies.

Edited by Gregory F. Augustine Pierce
Designed by John Dylong
Typography by LINK Book Development and Production
Artwork by Ann and Dick Rundall

Scripture selections taken from *The New American Bible with Revised New Testament,* copyright © 1986 by the Confraternity of Christian Doctrine, Washington, D.C., are used with permission. All rights reserved.
Scripture selections taken from *The New Jerusalem Bible,* copyright © 1985 by Darton, Longman & Todd, Ltd. and Doubleday & Company, Inc., New York, N.Y., are used with permission. All rights reserved.
All scriptural quotes are from *The New American Bible* unless noted as being from *The New Jerusalem Bible* by the annotation (JB) following the text.

Copyright © 1989: ACTA Publications
4848 N. Clark Street
Chicago, IL 60640
312-271-1030

Library of Congress Catalogue Number: 88-083578
ISBN: 0-9140706-61-4

Printed in the United States of America.

To Steve and Suzanne

Contents

PART III: DEATH AND RESURRECTION
AND THE GREAT DEATH   137

Acknowledgments

I WOULD LIKE TO EXPRESS MY DEEP GRATITUDE TO THE ABBOT AND THE NUNS AND MONKS OF THE Buddhist monastery of Wat Rempoeng near Chiang Mai, Thailand, for their gracious hospitality during my stay with them in August, 1986 and for their interest and care in initiating me into Theravada Buddhist meditation practice. I am also most grateful to John Daido Loori and the community at Zen Mountain Monastery in Mt. Tremper, N.Y., for their kind welcome during my visit in the spring of 1988. These meditations express my own efforts to understand, integrate, and apply the wisdom of Buddhist perspectives on life in light of the Christian tradition.

Many of the thoughts in these pages have found expression in homilies that I have delivered to the communities of Our Lady Help of Christians Church in Chicago, St. Patrick Church in Wadsworth, Illinois, and Mundelein Seminary in Mundelein, Illinois. To all of these congregations I express my appreciation for their attention and encouragement.

I would like to express my appreciation to a number of people who read earlier versions of these meditations and contributed greatly through their comments, suggestions, and criticisms. I especially thank Roger J. Corless of Duke University and two members of the Catholic Bishops' Committee for Ecumenical and Interreligious Affairs—John Borrelli, Executive Secretary of the Secretariat for Interreligious Relations and Eugene J. Fischer, Executive Secretary of the Secretariat for Catholic–Jewish Relations—for reading and commenting upon the manuscript. I also thank Wayne Prist, Louis Cameli, James McIlhone, John Shea—all of the University of Saint Mary of the Lake—as well as Gregory Pierce of ACTA Publications and Kenneth Trainor for their comments and suggestions. The weaknesses that remain are fully my own. I am especially grateful to John Shea for contributing the Foreword to this volume.

Foreword:
To Hear a Second
Time

A TWENTIETH CENTURY PUNDIT HAS REMARKED, "THE GOOD NEWS MAY BE GOOD BUT IT IS NOT news."

This quip about the basic Gospel message reflects a common contemporary malaise. It is a malaise that affects the entire biblical witness. This malaise is a weariness that has many names, but perhaps the most descriptive is "familiarization."

We have read or heard the biblical stories, prayers, proverbs, arguments, and reflections many times. We may not know what book of the Bible is being quoted, but references to Cain and Abel, David and Bathsheba, Judas's kiss and Peter's bitter weeping, "power is made perfect in weakness" and the "greatest of these is love" resonate in us. The Bible is the background book of western culture. Allusion to the Bible is one of the ways we interpret and communicate our experiences.

In other words, we are familiar with the Bible. We not only know the overall thrust of its content—from creation to the end of the world—but certain passages are immediately recognizable. Yet when we nod our heads in acknowledgment or yawn in boredom at a biblical passage, it is not only the Bible to which we are responding. Over the years associations have been attached to the various passages. Each biblical quotation is accompanied by a "standardized" theological interpretation. This traditional understanding of familiar texts is the mental package most of us carry around.

"A man went down from Jerusalem to Jericho," the preacher begins and we know that we are going to be encouraged to help the neighbor in need. "A woman taken in adultery" is presented to Jesus and we know we should not judge others because we too are sinners. No sooner do we hear that "a certain man had two sons" than we steel ourselves to struggle with God's unconditional forgiveness and its basic unfairness. We not only know the story, we also have a ready-made attached meaning.

Clergy often decry the biblical ignorance of the Christian people. And no doubt none of us knows the biblical witness well enough. But there is also a problem with biblical familiarity. What we do know about the Bible we have often "tamed with interpretation." We have so burdened certain texts with prescribed meanings that they cannot speak anew. We may not know the Bible well, but we know it well enough to think it has nothing more to say. Before we hear any of it we think we know all of it.

In this pastoral situation the task is not to evangelize or catechize but to "defamiliarize." Biblical texts are meant to challenge us. When they are the medium of the Word of God, they force us to see things differently, to ponder situations in a new way, to question where we never questioned before and to dare the answer and the action our timidity has always avoided. In order to do this—to be provocations of redemption—they cannot be as tame as a cat on our lap, as unobtrusive as parlor wallpaper. The well-worn, much-thumbed Bible must become a page-turner, a voyage of discovery.

This is no easy task.

But one way of defamiliarizing the text so that it can be heard in a new way is to bring a new conversation partner into the history of its interpretation. This new conversation partner will speak to the space between the text and its standard meanings, hear words and phrases previously overlooked or taken for granted, ask obvious questions that have never been asked before, and make suggestions that bring startling insights. In this way what we took to be old and thoroughly known becomes new and mysteriously evocative. When this happens, we may be in Paul Ricoeur's phrase "once more astonished."

Welcoming such a new conversation partner is what Leo Lefebure has done in this engaging book. He has facilitated a discussion between the "oxherds" and the "shepherds," creating a stimulating encounter between the Buddhist and Christian traditions. His way of doing this is to begin with a biblical text and allow it to dialogue with Buddhist insights into the self and salvation. The results are wonderful. The familiar texts speak new wisdom.

If with a sigh of tedium you think you have exhausted the meaning of the hierarchical ordering of creation in Genesis or the meaning of the little child in the teaching of Jesus; or if you think you understand

why it is wrong to look glum when fasting or what
exactly is the problem with the older brother; or if you
think you already know what the beloved disciple saw
when he peered into the emptiness of the tomb or why
Paul said he no longer lived but Christ lived in him; then
allow Leo Lefebure to turn the kaleidoscope of these
passages and many more into a new and stunning
mosaic.

This is a book for many different people.

If you pray with scripture but need a prod
beyond your own limited reflections and are frustrated
with consulting commentaries which ignore the religious feelings and perceptions of the texts, you have
found a spiritual companion in this book.

If you preach week in and week out, and week
in and week out you come up with the "same old stuff,"
welcome to "new stuff."

If you teach—on any level—and sense a need
for a more creative use of the biblical materials, you
have found it.

If you surmise that one sure direction for the
future of Christianity is in the dialogue with other
religious traditions, treat yourself to this concrete
example and then pat yourself on the back that your
surmise was correct.

With Leo Lefebure as our guide we can (in a
turn-of-phrase I hope would make both Christians and
Buddhists smile) hear the biblical texts for a second
time and, in the process, hear them for the first time.

—JOHN SHEA

Introduction

THE STORY OF A WEALTHY YOUNG PRINCE NAMED JOSAPHAT CIRCULATED THROUGHOUT EUROPE during the Middle Ages. According to the story, the young prince encountered a monk named Barlaam, an ascetic from the Sinai desert. The preaching of the monk so moved the young man that Josaphat asked to be baptized, renounced his claim to the throne, and went off into the desert to seek wisdom and truth in ascetic practice.

The story of Josaphat was told again and again all over medieval Europe, capturing the imaginations of people in Czechoslovakia, Poland, Russia, France, Germany, Spain, Sweden, Norway, and Iceland. The original person on whom the figure of Josaphat was based, however, was not a European. He was a prince from India. In fact, scholars have learned that his original name was not Josaphat and he never asked to be baptized as a Christian, but he was a prince and he did renounce his throne in order to search for wisdom.[1]

The medieval story of Josaphat was actually a re-telling of the story of Siddhartha Gautama, a wealthy young Indian prince who left his palace and power to seek enlightenment. He later came to be known as "Shakyamuni Buddha," that is, the Enlightened One of the Shakya clan.

At the time he left his palace, however, Siddhartha was not yet a Buddha; he was a future Buddha, or a "Bodhisattva." As his tale was told and re-told in one language after another, the name was altered again and again. The title, "Bodhisattva," became "Bodisaf" in the Manichean version of the tale, then "Yudasaf" in the Arabic version, then "Joasaph" in Greek, and eventually came to be identified with the biblical name, Josaphat or Jehoshaphat. When the story of the Buddha entered medieval Europe, it did so under the name of Josaphat.[2] Wilfred Cantwell Smith comments, "The historical fact is that, through this story, for a thousand years the Buddha *was* a Christian saint."[3]

For centuries, then, an adaptation of the story of the Buddha was honored as describing the life of a Christian saint. The influence of the Buddha on the Catholic imagination in medieval Europe is merely one example of the many ways in which Christians have enriched our own tradition by learning from other religious traditions.

The process of learning from other religious traditions is as old as the earliest writings of the Hebrew Bible. The writers of the Hebrew Bible used images of the Canaanite and Mesopotamian gods to describe the one God of Israel who led them out of Egypt. The wisdom teachers of Israel adapted material from Egyptian wisdom literature, such as "the Wisdom of Amen-em-ope," and incorporated it into the biblical Book of Proverbs. For centuries Christian thinkers interpreted the creation account in the Book of Genesis in light of Plato's description of the shaping of the world in the *Timaeus.*

As the contemporary world becomes ever more interconnected and interdependent, the process of learning from other religious traditions is accelerating, and its impact upon each tradition is deepening. It is increasingly difficult to understand any one religious tradition apart from others. While in the past some religious traditions developed in isolation from each other, the future promises ever increasing contacts among all religions in a pluralistic world.

To belong to a religious tradition in a pluralistic world challenges us to accept the responsibility of exploring our own heritage in dialogue with the other religious traditions of humankind. We understand our own or any tradition through listening to and interpreting its classic expressions, images, and stories. The path to understanding in a pluralistic world leads through the interpretation of the claims of differing religious classics. This means that it leads through dialogue.

To enter into genuine dialogue challenges us to listen to others' voices, to see the world through others' eyes, to break open the horizon of our own assumptions and pre-judgments. At the present time, the dialogue between Buddhists and Christians is introducing new perspectives and images into the awareness of Christians throughout the world. Precisely because Buddhist perspectives are so different from Christian views, they can make us aware of our own assumptions and help us to understand the resources and images of our own tradition in a fresh light.

Arnold Toynbee noted that for centuries Muslims and Christians have accepted the Jewish biblical tradition as part of their own religious self-understanding, and he expressed this hope: "I think one can foresee a time when the heritages of Islam and Buddhism will also have become part of the Christian society's background."[4]

The Second Vatican Council urged Catholic Christians "to enter with prudence and charity into discussion and collaboration with members of other religions."[5] More recently, in September, 1987, Pope John Paul II told a group of Zen monks:

> May all of you—partners in interreligious dialogue—be encouraged and sustained by the knowledge that your endeavors are supported by the Catholic Church and appreciated by her as significant for strengthening the bonds which unite all people who honestly search for the truth.[6]

The purpose of these meditations is to reflect upon the significance of biblical understandings of God and human life in dialogue with the images and perspectives of Mahayana Buddhist traditions of China and Japan. I offer these reflections in the hope that by listening to Buddhist voices Christians can re-hear our own Scriptures and re-cognize images of our own tradition with greater awareness and appreciation. My concern is more meditative than scholarly, and my style will be more homiletic than historical-critical. My goal is not to examine the original historical contexts of the texts that I am reflecting upon, but to compare and contrast the visions of life that are opened up by texts from these two traditions. Both the Christian and the Buddhist traditions have a long history of reflecting upon important images and stories in order to transform the lives of their hearers.

I am not suggesting that Christianity and Buddhism are saying the same thing. Nor am I seeking a common core or a new synthesis. The differences between these two traditions are so great that any synthesis at the present stage of dialogue would be premature. I am attempting to learn from Buddhist perspectives on human existence and, in light of them, to hear anew the voices of the Christian tradition.

One of the difficulties of comparing two traditions with as long and varied a history as Christianity and Buddhism is that there are radical differences within each tradition. Just as there is a variety of Christian points of view, so also there is no one Buddhist understanding of human existence but rather a wide variety of Buddhist perspectives which often conflict with each other. In these meditations I am reflecting from within the tradition of Catholic Christianity, and I am turning primarily to the Zen and Shin traditions of Mahayana Buddhism as they developed in China and Japan.[7]

At the center of both Zen and Shin Buddhism and Christianity is a process of transformation of our ordinary self. These traditions agree in seeing our ordinary self-understanding as distorted by selfishness, and they challenge us to change our awareness and behavior. The way this process is understood and nurtured is very different for each tradition, but both Christianity and Buddhism insist upon a radical transformation, a change that can be described as a "death" of the self that leads to true life.

Buddhists agree that the goal of the transformation of the self is wisdom and compassion, but Zen and Shin Buddhists approach this goal from rather different perspectives. Zen emphasizes self-power, reliance on one's own effort, while Shin relies on Other-Power, trust in the vow of the compassionate Amida Buddha to save all sentient beings. Many Buddhists, however, point out that the differences between the two approaches are not of ultimate importance. The teachings of self-power and Other-Power are not ends in themselves but rather "skilful means" whose purpose is to reach the goal of wisdom and compassion. Like all Buddhist teachings and practices, they are provisional means that are designed to transform human life. As one commentator noted, "As the beneficiaries become enlightened the expedients become redundant."[8] Buddhism in all its forms can be seen as a variety of skilful means offered by the Buddha and used by humans to transform human existence. In the experience of transformation, any division between self-power and Other-Power is ultimately overcome.

For the Christian tradition, the heart of the transformation of human life is the experience of faith, hope, and love. Faith, hope, and love are gifts of God that call forth human decisions. They summon us out of our ordinary patterns of living into a life centered on God. Faith, hope, and love constitute a process of self-surrender, a letting go of ourselves which is a radical acceptance of and submission to the reality of God.

Buddhists see insight into the emptiness of all reality as the key to wisdom and compassion. The Christian tradition itself has long cherished images of emptiness, though in a very different sense of the term. St. Paul described the incarnation as Christ's emptying of himself (Philippians 2:7). From the call of Jesus to self-sacrifice to his death on the cross, the Christian heritage confronts us with powerful images of self-emptying. Even though the meanings of wisdom and emptiness in the Bible are radically different from Buddhist understandings, we can attempt to learn from each other's understandings and interpret Buddhist and Christian images in light of each other.

Since I am writing primarily for Christians who are interested in exploring their tradition in relation to Buddhist perspectives, each section of this book will begin by introducing Buddhist images and understandings as a preparation for reflecting upon biblical passages. I would, of course, hope that a Buddhist might find something of value in these meditations as well.

These meditations will move through three stages. Both Christian and Buddhist understandings of human existence presuppose visions of the universe in which we make our decisions. The first section of the meditations will explore biblical understandings of creation in light of Buddhist images of the cosmos. A variety of biblical passages describe the creation of the world, the relation of wisdom to creation and to humans, and the relation of Christ to the cosmos. While the most familiar accounts of creation are those of the opening chapters of Genesis, many other passages in the Bible also describe the relation of God to the world. The wisdom tradition—represented by the books of Proverbs, Job, Ecclesiastes, Sirach, and Wisdom—gives particular attention to the meaning of creation. The perspectives of Job and Ecclesiastes radically challenge other perspectives present within the biblical tradition and offer some suggestive comparisons and contrasts to Buddhist perspectives on human existence and the cosmos.

The second section will explore the search for the true self in Christianity and Buddhism. The Zen and Shin traditions of Buddhism offer strikingly different views on the way the search should proceed. The Zen tradition has emphasized sitting meditation and the use of *koans* (paradoxical questions or sayings) to transform human consciousness. In Zen Buddhism there is a famous series of ten drawings or paintings that represent an oxherd searching for an ox. The drawings dramatize the oxherd's search for and discovery of his true self, which is empty. The Shin tradition of Buddhism is skeptical of reliance on human efforts and trusts in the compassionate vow of Amida Buddha.

In the biblical tradition humans often appear to be searching for God, but the search goes two ways, for God is also searching for us. In the Book of Exodus it is God who takes the initiative in offering commandments to structure Israel's life in the covenant. One of the best-known images of the parables of Jesus is that of the Good Shepherd who cares for his sheep and goes out searching for the one lost sheep. Throughout the Bible questions of human identity in relation to God and questions about the proper way to find oneself and God abound. The search for our true self involves wrestling with the significance of religious actions, of commandments, of our own self-understanding.

In both Christianity and Buddhism the search for the self involves a loss of self and a rediscovery of a deeper level of existence. The third section will examine Christian images of death and resurrection in dialogue with Buddhist understandings of the "Great Death," which is the experience of enlightenment. For both Buddhists and Christians, the death of the self is a transformation leading to fuller, more authentic life.

Life Transformed

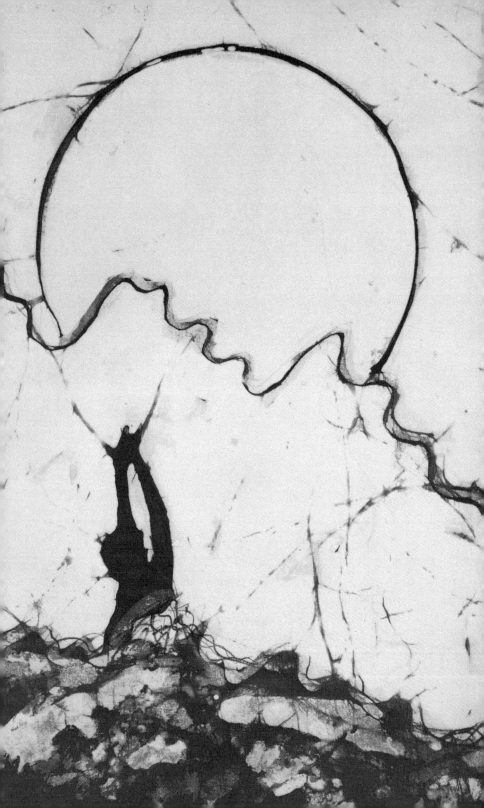

PART I

Cosmic Visions: The Economy of Gift and the Jewel-Net of Indra

I MPORTANT TO BOTH CHRISTIANITY AND BUDDHISM IS THE UNDERSTANDING OF THE COSMIC stage upon which we act out our lives. The Christian understanding of the cosmos is expressed through the doctrine of creation, which expresses the dependence of all finite realities upon God. To place creation at the center of a Christian perspective is to give a central role to the experience of all things as gift. It means inscribing all our acting and being within what Paul Ricoeur has called the "economy of gift."9

To view the world as creation is to highlight the acceptance of our lives and our world from a power we do not control and cannot manipulate. From the gift of our lives and our world there arise responsibilities and obligations to ourselves and those around us. The book of Genesis tells of God creating various forms of life and entrusting the garden of Eden to humankind "to cultivate and care for it" (2:15). The Book of Proverbs personifies the ordering power of creation as Lady Wisdom, a gracious woman who is the way in which humans experience God (8:1–36). Lady Wisdom plays before God at the creation of the world, finds delight in humankind, and calls humans to find life, happiness, and favor by following her counsel and discipline (Proverbs 8:31–36).

The early Christian community's experience of revelation and salvation in Jesus Christ led them to reflect upon the meaning of creation in light of Christ. Hymns in the New Testament use the language earlier used for Lady Wisdom to describe Christ as the one through whom all things were created, the one in whom all things hold together (Colossians 1:17; John 1:1–5). For the Christian community, the meaning of creation is revealed in the account of the life, death, and resurrection of Jesus, the incarnation of Lady Wisdom.

The doctrine of creation does not mean that God is simply set over against the world. The Christian tradition has long stressed that God is not only transcendent of but also immanent in all finite realities. As Augustine put it, God is in all things and all things are in God: "I should be null and void and could not exist at all, if you, my God, were not in me. Or is it rather that I should not exist, unless I existed in you?"[10] Creator and creation interpenetrate one another.

Buddhist perspectives on the world are quite different. Buddhist understandings of the cosmos do not begin from the activity of a creative God, and Buddhists are skeptical of any speculation about cosmic origins that appears to go beyond the bounds of experience. Speculation on the nature of creation can itself be a cause of pain and sorrow. The Buddha himself refused to answer questions about the origin of the world, stressing that they would not answer the pressing question of understanding and eliminating human suffering. There is, nonetheless, a long tradition of Buddhist imagery which portrays the type of world we live in.

One of the favorite Buddhist images to describe the way the universe exists is the jewel-net of Indra.[11] Indra was a Hindu God from very ancient times in India. What Hua-yen and Zen Buddhists in China and Japan remember most about Indra is his great net that has been hung across the universe, stretching out to infinity in every direction. At every crossing of the net, each eye has a sparkling jewel. Since the net stretches out to infinity, there is no limit to the number of jewels it contains. If one looks very closely, one can see that each jewel reflects every other jewel in the net.

The net represents the cosmos, and the jewels in the net are all the beings in the cosmos. The image of the jewel-net suggests that we live in mutual interdependence with every other being in the universe. Every other being has an effect upon us, and we have an effect upon every other being, no matter how slight that effect may be. The stars on the other side of the universe affect us, and we affect them. To exist is to reflect every other being, and to be reflected in every other being.

During the T'ang Dynasty of China, the Chinese Empress Wu Tse-T'ien was struggling to comprehend the Buddhist understanding which had come from India. To illustrate this vision of the universe, the Chinese Buddhist philosopher Fa-Tsang (643–712) proposed another image parallel to the jewel-net of Indra: he set up an image of the Buddha next to a burning torch in the middle of a hall with mirrors on each wall, the ceiling, and the floor. The mirrors reflected the

Buddha's image countless times on every side. The reflections in turn reflected the other reflections in a play of images without end. Fa-Tsang explained:

> In each and every reflection of any mirror you will find all the reflections of all the other mirrors, together with the specific Buddha image in each, without omission or misplacement. The principle of interpenetration and containment is clearly shown by this demonstration. Right here we see an example of one in all and all in one.[12]

According to this vision, the entire universe depends upon us, for it would not be the universe it is if we were not who we are. In turn, we depend upon the entire universe, for we would not be who we are if every being in the universe were not what it is. There is a constant mutual causality between us and every other being in the universe. Buddhists describe the relationship as one of both identity and interdependence. We are one with every other being through this interdependence, this sharing in the one great jewel-net of Indra.

The Japanese Shingon Buddhist teacher, Kukai (774–835), known posthumously as Kobo Daishi, interpreted the image of the jewel-net of Indra to mean:

> Existence is my existence, the existence of the Buddhas, and the existences of all sentient beings. . . . All of these existences are interrelated horizontally and vertically without end, like images in mirrors, or like the rays of lamps. This existence is in that one, and that one is in this.[13]

In such a universe, relationships are of central importance, for our relationships to all other beings make us who we are. Relationships are not somehow added to beings that already exist by themselves. Rather, relationships are the way we exist. The thought that we exist independently by ourselves is a fundamental delusion in Buddhism, a delusion that works tremendous harm: it is the root cause of our selfish desires and our suffering. Our desires deceive us into making ourselves the center of the universe and tempt us to make everything else a means to serving our deluded self.

Buddhists use the term *shunyata* (emptiness) to describe the way things exist. To say all things are empty means that they do not sustain themselves. Things come to be through a process that Buddhists call dependent co-arising: the process of each being arising in dependence upon a network of other beings, the process of belonging to the jewel-net of Indra. Nothing exists by itself alone. There is no inherently existing, self-sufficient substance, no "self-made" individual that does not exist in interdependence with all other people and beings in the universe. Since all things without exception are interdependent, all relationships are reciprocal.

To realize that things are empty means to see them as they are, apart from the distortions of our desires and delusions. To see things as empty means to experience things "just-as-they-are." This is what Buddhists call "suchness." Emptiness or suchness is the truth of ourselves and the universe in which we live. When we let go of the delusion of our independent, self-sufficient existence and the distorting lens of our ego-centered desires, then we allow things to be just what they are—and they can enlighten us.

For Buddhists, wisdom is insight into the emptiness of all things and of ourselves; it is the letting go of any concept of ourselves as substantial and self-sufficient. Wisdom is the awareness of the mutual interdependence and mutual causality that links us to every other being. With wisdom comes compassion, the concern not only for all humans but for all beings whatsoever. Wisdom involves identification with all beings.

We realize that we do not profit by another's loss; our selfishness hurts ourselves. Since we live in a universe of interpenetration and interdependence, to value one's ego as the center of a world of desires is to live in a delusion that leads inevitably to much suffering for oneself and others.

For Buddhists, the interdependence and identity of all beings means that there is no inherently existing self, and also no God: there is no divine reality upon whom all things depend. The jewel-net of Indra is not created by any transcendent divine plan or any divine giver. Buddhism claims not to be atheist in the modern Western sense but rather non-theist. It does not deny God, but neither does it rely on God. As D. T. Suzuki (1870–1966) put it, "in Zen, God is neither denied nor insisted upon."[14]

Even though Buddhists do not interpret the universe in relation to a creating God, Shin Buddhists in particular do emphasize the experience of the universe as gift. The Japanese Shin Buddhist Manshi Kiyozawa (1863–1903) stressed the experience of awe and trust in the working of the Infinite Other-Power. He noted the wonder of the cosmos and lamented our ignoring it:

> The countless myriads of events that make up the cosmos all belong to the wondrous doing of the one Great Miracle. And yet we take the whole spectacle as if it were quite ordinary and matter of course. The reverence and esteem it ought to inspire in us is stillborn.[15]

He continued: "The glow of a color, the fragrance of a scent, these things can never come to be of their own power. They cannot exist without relying on the power of the one Great Miracle. . . . The hand of the Other-Power has us absolutely in its palm."[16] The proper response to the gift of ourselves and our world, according to Kiyozawa, is a trusting gratitude and awe.

☐ *Then God said:*
"Let us make man in our image, after our likeness.
Let them have dominion over the fish of the sea,
the birds of the air, and the cattle,
and over all the wild animals
and all the creatures that crawl on the ground."

God created man in his image;
  in the divine image he created him;
  male and female he created them.

God blessed them saying:
"Be fertile and multiply; fill the earth and subdue it.
Have dominion over the fish of the sea,
the birds of the air,
and all the living things that move on the earth."

God also said:
"See, I give you every seed-bearing plant all over the
earth and every tree that has seed-bearing fruit on it
to be your food; and to all the animals of the land,
all the birds of the air,
and all the living creatures that crawl on the ground,
I give all the green plants for food."

And so it happened.
God looked at everything he had made,
and he found it very good. ☐

(Genesis 1:26–31)

1 The Creation of Humanity and the World

A̲T THE HEART OF BIBLICAL UNDERSTANDINGS OF CREATION IS THE ACCEPTANCE OF OUR WORLD and our own selves as a gift. At the core of our identity is the gift of our very selves. From this gift arise our obligations. As Jesus would put it, "Much will be required of the person entrusted with much, and still more will be demanded of the person entrusted with more" (Luke 12:48).

The two creation accounts at the beginning of Genesis balance the special position of humans in the world with humankind's responsibilities to care for the rest of creation. Only humans are created in the image of God, and God entrusts humans with dominion over fish, birds, and animals. Human dominion over nature is not unrestricted, however: the first humans are to eat only of the plants of the earth (not until after the flood will God allow humans to eat every living creature [Genesis 9:3]). God's care extends to all creation, for

God makes provision for other creatures' food as well. The command of God to humans to fill the earth and subdue it involves obligations to care for the earth. While the Christian tradition has often paid great attention to the creation of humans in the image of God, the Jewish tradition has remembered that in Genesis the summit of creation is not the creation of humans but the Sabbath rest on the seventh day.

The second account of creation in Genesis (2:4b–25) also balances the privileges of humans with their obligations. The first man is settled in the garden of Eden "to cultivate and care for it" (2:15). He gives names to the birds and animals, and thus, in the context of the ancient Near East, exercises a certain sovereignty over them parallel to the dominion in Genesis 1:28. The divine intent, however, is for harmony among the various creatures, a harmony that will be broken through the trickery of the serpent and human disobedience (3:14–19).

While the best of the Christian tradition has followed the book of Genesis and insisted upon proper human responsibility and stewardship for nature, in the modern period Christians have sometimes allowed the biblical commandment of dominion to be distorted into a justification for abusing nature without respect. The commission to subdue nature has been seen as reinforcing the approach of modern science to nature as an object to be manipulated and controlled.

The Buddhist universe contrasts sharply with the accounts of creation in Genesis. There is no Buddhist narrative of the beginning of the universe. When asked about the beginning of time, Shakyamuni Buddha insisted that no starting point of time could be known. Speculation about such matters would only reinforce our delusions and add to suffering. For Buddhists, there is no divine decision to fashion a world and create different forms of life one after the other.

While in Buddhist perspectives humans are not created in the image of a Creator, humans do, nonetheless, have a special responsibility in the cosmos because of our consciousness and our greater possibility of making choices that affect all beings. As humans, we can become aware of the cause of suffering and can eliminate it. For Buddhists, there is a strong sense of solidarity with the cosmos and of mutual interdependence among all beings throughout the universe, and so each human person's experience of enlightenment affects all together.

Buddhists distinguish two ways of relating to nature: we can analyze nature as an object that we seek to understand and control or we can realize that we are not separate from all beings and allow the things of the universe to enlighten us. The first way gives us a certain mastery and power over processes of nature, but if we mistake it for genuine enlightenment, it is a delusion. The Japanese Zen teacher Dogen (1200–1253) commented: "That the self advances and confirms the myriad things is called delusion; that the myriad things advance and confirm the self is enlightenment."[17]

Dogen described the way of enlightenment in a famous passage:

> To study the Way is to study the self. To study the self is to forget the self. To forget the self is to be enlightened by all things of the universe. To be enlightened by all things of the universe is to cast off the body and mind of the self as well as those of others. Even the traces of enlightenment are wiped out, and life with traceless enlightenment goes on forever and ever.[18]

In enlightenment we realize that we are not separate from the universe, we see the idea of a separate, inherently existing self as a delusion, and we allow the myriad things around us to enlighten us. To be enlightened by all the things of the universe means that we gain a new perspective on the world, a point of view from which all dualities and separations are seen as empty. Enlightenment does not bring a new intellectual theory about the universe but a new way of experiencing the universe.

According to Dogen, the *Dharma* (the Truth, the teaching of the Buddha) is already present within each of us, but we only realize it through practice, especially through *zazen* (sitting meditation). Dogen explained that for the person practicing zazen, there is a mutual process of enlightening the myriad things and being enlightened by them:

> Trees and grasses, wall and fence expound and exalt the Dharma for the sake of ordinary people, sages, and all living beings. Ordinary people, sages, and all living beings in turn preach and exalt the Dharma for the sake of trees, grasses, wall and fence.[19]

For Dogen, there is no enlightenment of oneself without enlightening others: the person practicing zazen becomes one with every being in the cosmos and so one's own enlightenment is one with the enlightenment of all beings. To cast off one's own mind and body is also to cast off those of others. But even this new state is not to be grasped at as a possession: "even the traces of enlightenment are wiped out."

D. T. Suzuki explained that in this experience the world is changed:

> [T]he world for those who have gained a satori [enlightenment] is no more the old world as it used to be; even with all its flowing streams and burning fires, it is never the same one again. Logically stated, all its opposites and contradictions are united and harmonized into a consistent organic whole.[20]

Christians have often interpreted the biblical accounts of creation as suggesting that humans are set over against the rest of creation, and Christian understandings of salvation have usually concentrated primarily upon the redemption of human beings. The Buddhist insistence on the mutual interdependence of all beings can be a strong stimulus to remember the harmony among all creatures intended by God in Genesis. In light of the tremendous destructive power of modern technology over nature, Buddhist perspectives present a forceful and needed challenge to modern Western self-understandings that take an aggressive, manipulative approach to nature.

Dogen's emphasis on the unity of human enlightenment and the enlightenment of all beings may seem strange at first. Christians often do not think of non-human creatures as being saved. St. Paul, however, is quite clear that redemption does not affect humans alone but involves the entire cosmos:

> [F]or the whole creation is waiting with eagerness for the children of God to be revealed. It was not for its own purposes that creation had frustration imposed on it, but for the purposes of him who imposed it—with the intention that the whole creation itself might be freed from its slavery to corruption and brought into the same glorious freedom as the children of God (Romans 8:19-21; JB).

☐ *God said to Noah and to his sons with him:*
"See, I am now establishing my covenant
with you and your descendents after you
and with every living creature
that was with you:
all the birds,
and the various tame and wild animals
that were with you and came out of the ark. . . ."

God added:
"This is the sign that I am giving
for all ages to come,
of the covenant between me and you
and every living creature with you:
I set my bow in the clouds
to serve as a sign of the covenant
between me and the earth." ☐

(Genesis 9:8–10, 12–13)

2 A Covenant with the Earth

T HE CHAPTERS OF GENESIS THAT FOLLOW THE CREATION ACCOUNTS TELL OF THE APPEARANCE and spread of sin over the earth. Humans refuse to accept the harmony with other creatures that God wills. Human arrogance, pride, and violence form a network of sin that entraps all humankind and does violence to the earth itself. While Christians have often thought of sin as primarily affecting human existence, in the book of Genesis the process of corruption and punishment is specially caused by humans but involves all living creatures:

> God looked at the earth; it was corrupt, for corrupt were the ways of all living things on earth. God said to Noah, "I have decided that the end has come for all living things, for the earth is full of lawlessness because of human beings. So I am now about to destroy them and the earth" (Genesis 6:11-13; JB).

God is on the verge of destroying creation altogether, but decides to attempt a new beginning. Just as corruption and punishment affect all the earth, so too does the covenant that God makes after the destructive power of the flood has ebbed. Christians have often tended to think that God's covenants are with human beings. In practice we often think of ourselves as the creatures that God cares about. It is striking, however, that after the flood God shows deep concern not only for humans but for all forms of life. The covenant that God makes after the flood is not only with Noah and his family but with the earth and with all living creatures. There is a profound solidarity between humans and the rest of creation—a solidarity which is sanctified in the covenant between God and all creation.

For Buddhists, the problem of human existence also has to be understood in relation to the entire cosmos. In Buddhist visions of the universe all sentient beings are joined in suffering because all are subject to birth-and-death. Even more fundamental than the problem of birth-and-death is the condition of appearance and disappearance of all beings in the universe. In the flow of experience things are constantly arising and disappearing. What appears to be a stationary object is actually a series of individual moments. There is no thing that lasts permanently. Everything is empty.

The problem of human existence for Buddhists is not rebellion against a creating God but rather ignorance of the true condition, the impermanence of all things. Because we cling to the erroneous idea of an inherently existing self, we cling to desires, striving to possess the "things" that we perceive around us. The result is very close to the situation described by the book of Genesis: human arrogance and selfishness do grave damage to the quality of life for all beings. The network of delusion spreads further and further in an inexorable cycle of violence and suffering.

While Christians have developed theories of original sin to interpret the problem of human existence going awry, Buddhists have used the term "ignorance" (*avidya*). Ignorance is the inability to see things as they are, as impermanent, and it is the root of the evil passions that delude the mind and body and poison the atmosphere of life. For the Buddhist tradition, ignorance, anger, and greed are the three poisons that hold sway over life apart from enlightenment. The resolution of the problem for Buddhists is to see all things, including ourselves, in their suchness, as arising and disappearing. When we do so, we are freed from the dominating control of our passions.

Where the book of Genesis finds reconciliation in a new divine initiative that invites humans to live in covenant with God and all creation, Buddhists look for a new harmony with all beings after awakening. In both traditions human reconciliation involves a new relationship to all other beings. Buddhists recount that when Shakyamuni Buddha was enlightened, he realized that all beings shared together in enlightenment. Traditional Buddhist sayings proclaim: "All the trees and herbs and lands attain Buddhahood," and "Mountains and rivers and the earth all disclose their *Dharmakaya* [essential Buddhahood]."²¹

In Genesis the covenant with creation after the flood is God's voluntary self-limiting: God promises not to use/abuse creation to punish human evil in this way again. God is withdrawing from certain uses of power, allowing a space in which various forms of life can develop, and God challenges humans to do likewise. Buddhists strongly agree that human power must be used within strict limits with an awareness of the solidarity of all beings in the cosmos. For Buddhists, the challenge comes not from a divine covenant but from the demands of their own awareness. The responsible use of power flows from awakening to the truth.

□ *Then from the heart of the tempest*
Yahweh gave Job his answer. He said:
"Who is this obscuring my intentions
  with his ignorant words?

Brace yourself like a fighter;
  I am going to ask the questions,
  and you are to inform me!

Where were you when I laid the earth's foundations?
Tell me, since you are so well-informed! . . .

Have you visited the place where the snow is stored?
  Have you seen the stores of hail,
which I keep for times of distress,
  for days of battle and war?

From which direction does the lightning fork,
  where in the world does the east wind
  blow itself out?

Who bores a channel for the downpour
  or clears the way for the rolling thunder
so that rain may fall on lands where no one lives,
  and the deserts void of human dwelling,
to meet the needs of the lonely wastes
  and make grass sprout on the thirsty ground?" □

(Job 38:1–4, 22–27; JB)

3 The Voice from the Tempest

T HE BOOK OF JOB OFFERS A VERY SHARP CRITIQUE OF ANY ANTHROPOCENTRIC VIEW OF THE UNI-verse. Overwhelmed by his pain, Job had cried out for God to answer him. The resolution of Job's quest for justice is not a direct answer to the questions he asked of God. When God speaks from the whirlwind, God does not explain the reason for undeserved human suffering. Instead, God refers to the order in the cosmos, an order which humans can only partially comprehend. The implication seems to be that just as there is an order in the physical universe which humans can only partially grasp, so also in the moral universe there is an order which surpasses human judgment.

God reminds Job that the universe was not created for human pleasure and control. The book of Job offers a rather different perspective from that of Genesis, where humans are commanded to exercise dominion over other forms of life. In the book of Job, humans cannot even fathom the wonders of the world and the variety of forms of creatures, let alone have dominion over them.

The Buddhist image of Indra's jewel-net also describes a universe which is not centered around the human person, a universe which is interpenetrating and interdependent. For Buddhists, instead, everything requires everything else to be what it is. In the Buddhist universe there is no hierarchy or center. Rather, the center is everywhere.

The striking contrast, of course, is that Job encounters a God who consciously designed the order of the universe, whereas in the Buddhist universe there is no transcendent creator. Even this important difference should not be overstated, however. Shin Buddhists do have a very strong sense of absolute dependence upon Other-Power as the source from which they and all things in the universe arise.

Kiyozawa asked: "Where is it, this Infinite Other-Power? You may see it in what you yourself have received. Everything you have received is an apparition of the Infinite Other-Power. Honor it. Treasure it."[22] The proper response to this gift is grateful awe: "So it is not for us to grieve or to rejoice in the face of life and death. . . . Better we should simply stand in awe of the works of this wondrous Other-Power among all the myriad events of the cosmos."[23]

In the divine speeches to Job, in the image of the jewel-net of Indra and in the Shin Buddhist sense of Other-Power, there is a process of "decentering" the human place in the universe. We learn that we are not the center of the universe, and we lose our usual frame of reference. In each tradition, this decentering leads to a reconciliation and union in peace. Job accepts the revelation of God and finds his peace; the Buddhist, upon accepting her or his place in the jewel-net of Indra, in gratefully trusting in Other-Power, is in harmony with all beings.

☐ I, Wisdom, share house with Discretion,
  I am mistress of the art of thought. . . .
Yahweh created me, first-fruits of his fashioning,
  before the oldest of his works.
From everlasting, I was firmly set,
  from the beginning, before the earth came into being.
The deep was not, when I was born,
  nor were the springs with their abounding waters. . . .
When he fixed the heavens firm, I was there,
  when he drew a circle on the surface of the deep,
when he thickened the clouds above,
  when the sources of the deep began to swell,
when he assigned the sea its boundaries—
  and the waters will not encroach on the shore—
  when he traced the foundations of the earth,
I was beside the master craftsman,
  delighting him day after day,
  ever at play in his presence,
at play everywhere on his earth,
  delighting to be with the children of men.
And now, my children, listen to me.
  Happy are those who keep my ways.
Listen to instruction and become wise,
  do not reject it.
Blessed, whoever listens to me,
  who day after day keeps watch at my gates
  to guard my portals.
For whoever finds me finds life,
  and obtains the favor of Yahweh;
but whoever misses me harms himself,
  all who hate me are in love with death. ☐

(Proverbs 8:12; 22–24, 27–36; JB)

4 The Play of Lady Wisdom

F OR BUDDHISTS, WISDOM MEANS UNDERSTAND-
ING THE PLACE WE OCCUPY WITHIN THE JEWEL-
net of Indra, that is, our relationships to all beings.
Wisdom means allowing things to be just as they are,
without distorting them through our desires. Wisdom
means realizing suchness, that is, experiencing all
things such as they are. At root, wisdom is awakening to
nonduality.

> In the higher realm of true Suchness
> There is neither "self" nor "other":
> When direct identification is sought,
> We can only say, "Not two."[24]

In becoming wise, we see all distinctions and
divisions as—in the end—empty, and we are one with all
things. Wisdom is not a new theory about reality but
seeing through the delusory self which is the source of
suffering. Wisdom breaks through the chains of our
ordinary discriminating consciousness and sets us free

to be our true selves. Our ordinary thinking makes distinctions between one thing and another. Buddhist wisdom is sometimes called "beyond thinking" or "no-thinking" because it passes beyond analysis and distinctions. In wisdom there is no separation between knower and known. As Douglas Fox has put it, for Buddhists, "wisdom is not something we acquire, but something we discover ourselves to *be*."[25]

Even though wisdom is not discovered outside ourselves, Buddhists do describe the experience of wisdom as a gift, and they have personified the source of wisdom as a woman who enlightens human hearts. One version of the Heart Sutra begins by proclaiming: "Honor to the Lady, Noble Transcendent Wisdom."[26] Buddhists in southern India speak of Wisdom as "the Mother of the Victorious," meaning the mother of the Buddhas. One Buddhist text proclaims:

> Perfect Wisdom spreads her radiance . . . and is worthy of worship. Spotless, the whole world cannot stain her. . . . In her we may find refuge; her works are most excellent; she brings us to safety under the sheltering wings of enlightenment. . . . She is omniscience; without beginning or end is Perfect Wisdom, who has Emptiness as her characteristic mark.[27]

The Bible also personifies the source of wisdom as a woman who enlightens humans. The biblical wisdom tradition presents Lady Wisdom as the power of order that holds all things in the universe together. In Proverbs 8 she plays at the side of God in creation, delighting God and playing with humans. As Lady Wisdom plays before God, the world comes into being. The book of Proverbs suggests that creation itself arises as an act of playful and spontaneous delight.

Lady Wisdom is a poetic expression of the way in which humans experience the movement of God throughout human life and the cosmos. In the ancient wisdom tradition, Lady Wisdom appears as the form in which God influences the world and in which God wishes to be sought by humankind. In later Christian reflection Lady Wisdom came to be identified with the divine Word which was incarnate in Jesus, and eventually with the Second Person of the Christian Trinity. The figure of Lady Wisdom is a way of naming the reality of God's love that is at work throughout the cosmos and within ourselves.

In the Bible, Lady Wisdom appears as playful, but her play with humans is deadly serious, for she confronts us with a decision and it is our own lives that are at stake in her call. To accept brings life; to reject brings death. The Buddhist poet Rahulabhadra (ca. 150–200) described Perfect Wisdom as also showing two faces to those she encounters:

> When as fearful Thou appearest
> Thou engender'st fear in fools;
> When benignly Thou appearest
> Comes assurance to the wise.[28]

The Wisdom of Solomon describes Lady Wisdom as both "a reflection of the eternal light, untarnished mirror of God's active power" (7:26) and also as penetrating the entire universe: "she is so pure, she pervades and permeates all things" (7:24). She is "a breath of the power of God" (7:25) who passes into humans, making them "into God's friends and prophets" (7:27). Lady Wisdom is the power overcoming divisions, uniting God and humans. She is the source of the prophets' inspiration.

Buddhists also experience Perfect Wisdom as a woman who is the source of grace and compassion. It is she who sends Buddhas into the world to enlighten us:

> Teachers of the world, the Buddhas,
> Are Thine own compassionate sons;
> Then art Thou, O Blessed Lady,
> Grandam thus of beings all.[29]

In both the Buddhist and the biblical descriptions, Wisdom is always already present throughout the cosmos, even though she is often not recognized by humans. The biblical Lady Wisdom has been playing in creation since the beginning, and yet humans consistently refuse to recognize her (Proverbs 1:20-33). Rahulabhadra notes a similar paradox in the Buddhist experience:

> Wonderful, profound, illustrious,
> Hard Thou art to recognize.
> Like a mock show Thou art seen, and
> Yet Thou art not seen at all.[30]

In both traditions the encounter with Lady Wisdom can teach us the truth of the cosmos and of ourselves and thus bring us reconciliation. Buddhist descriptions of wisdom differ from the biblical tradition most strikingly in their insistence on the complete identity of wisdom and ourselves. Even though Buddhist wisdom is experienced as a gift coming from a gracious feminine figure, Buddhist wisdom is emptiness, and it is ultimately not other than ourselves. Biblical wisdom is received as a gift from God, a gift that has always been offered to us; the heart of Buddhist wisdom is the awakening to what we have always possessed.

□ *Sheer futility, Qoheleth says.*
Sheer futility: everything is futile!
What profit can we show for all our toil,
toiling under the sun?
A generation goes, a generation comes,
yet the earth stands firm for ever. . . .

I, Qoheleth, have reigned over Israel
in Jerusalem.
Wisely I have applied myself to investigation
and exploration of everything
that happens under heaven.
What a wearisome task God has given humanity
to keep us busy!
I have seen everything that is done under the sun;
how futile it all is,
mere chasing after the wind!

I know there is no happiness for a human being
except in pleasure and enjoyment through life.
And when we eat and drink
and find happiness in all our achievements,
this is a gift from God. □

(Ecclesiastes 1:2–4, 12–14; 3:12–13; JB)

5 Vanity and Emptiness

A BUDDHIST MONK, SEEING A WITHERED LEAF FALL FROM A TREE, AWAKENED TO THE IMPERMANENCE of the total universe, including himself.[31] The Buddhist saw all things as *shunya* (empty), as insubstantial, and was enlightened.

At the conclusion of the Diamond Sutra, Shakyamuni Buddha advises his listeners:

> All composite things
> Are like a dream, a phantasm, a bubble, and a shadow,
> Are like a dew-drop and a flash of lightning;
> They are thus to be regarded.[32]

The refrain of impermanence echoes again and again in Buddhist thought. The result of realizing the transience and insubstantiality of all things is not a pessimistic despair, but rather a sense of liberation, a freedom from a false notion of one's self, and thus a greater concern for others. Dogen advised his students:

> Do good for others, without thinking of making yourself known so that you may gain reward. Really bring benefit to

others, gaining nothing for yourself. . . . To establish such
an attitude, you must first understand impermanence. Our
life is like a dream, and time passes swiftly.[33]

Qoheleth, the author of the book of Ecclesiastes (the word *Qoheleth* in Hebrew means "the one
who calls the assembly," or "the preacher"), also has a
strong sense of the emptiness of all things and the
transience of all pursuits in this world. All things are
sheer futility! The Hebrew word *hebel* (sheer futility),
which is often translated as "vanity," literally means
"vapor" or "breath." It describes what is evanescent
and unsubstantial. The word comes close to what Buddhists mean by saying all things are empty.

Qoheleth, like much Buddhist thought, is
obsessed by the vanity, the transience, the emptiness of
our existence. His conclusion is close to the Buddhist's:
we are not to worry about matters in the past or future
that are beyond our power, but rather should live in the
present and enjoy our present work and relationships.
In spite of the suffering caused by the ravages of time,
Qoheleth affirms: "And therefore I praise joy" (8:15;
JB).

Zen Buddhists have a perspective on time that
in some ways is rather similar. Qoheleth advises:

The past is out of reach,
buried deep—who can discover it? (7:24; JB).

A Zen master warns us: "Let not things of the
past possess your mind. The past is past, do not pursue
it, and the past mind ceases by itself. This is said to be
cutting off all past affairs. The things of the future are not
here yet."[34] The outcome of Buddhist enlightenment is
not a world-weary pessimism but an intense enjoyment
of the present moment. The Chinese Zen layman, P'ang-
yün exclaimed:

How wondrously supernatural,
And how miraculous this!
I draw water, and I carry fuel![35]

Having let go of the false anxieties of the past
and the future, the Zen Buddhist, like Qoheleth, can live
more deeply in the present.

☐ *When those who had started about five o'clock*
came, each received the usual daily wage.

> *So when the first came,*
> *they thought that they would receive more,*
> *but each of them also got the usual wage.*

And on receiving it they grumbled
against the landowner, saying,

> *"These last ones worked only one hour,*
> *and you have made them equal to us,*
> *who bore the day's burden*
> *and the heat."*

He said to one of them in reply,

> *"My friend I am not cheating you.*
> *Did you not agree with me*
> *for the usual daily wage? . . .*

Are you envious because I am generous?" ☐

(Matthew 20:9–13,15)

6 Are You Envious Because I Am Generous?

R| ECEIVING A GIFT CAN BE A SOURCE OF GREAT JOY AND ALSO OF GREAT ENVY. GIFTS CAN HAVE A powerful impact upon both the giver and receiver. While they can create important bonds uniting people, gifts can also have a strange way of dividing a group of people, creating animosities and jealous comparisons. To live in an economy of gift can be deeply unsettling.

Giving appears as a threat to the early morning workers in Jesus's parable. Indeed, the conclusion of Jesus's story must have seemed like a cruel joke to those who worked all day. They, after all, had been up early and had worked through the hot sun. Then they had to endure the indignity of having to wait at the end of the line and watch as those who came in late and worked only an hour were paid first. It seems almost as if the owner was deliberately setting them up to expect something more, and so it must have come like a slap in

47

the face when they were paid the same as the latecomers.

The complaint of those who worked all through the day lurks inside each of us. Given the proper circumstances, it will leap out almost in spite of ourselves: "That's not fair!" We protest someone else's good fortune when we think that we deserved better.

Jesus's story is a direct response to the complaint, but it offers no answer in the usual sense. Instead, Jesus answers a question with a question: "Are you envious because I am generous?"

Jesus launches a direct assault on the presupposition of the complaint, on the entire system of reward and punishment as a guide to our relationship to God. In so doing, he undermines the ordinary sense of the self. Jesus does not deny that the system of reward and punishment has its claims. The owner in the parable protests that he is not unjust. Jesus, however, inscribes the system of reward and punishment within a larger system, an economy of gift which is not based upon merit and demerit but upon the generosity of God.

The generosity of God is precisely what we cannot predict or control. Jesus's counter-question to the workers is an invitation to let go of comparisons, to let go of the nagging worry about who received how much. It is a challenge to enter a different frame of reference, one based not on merit and demerit but on the overwhelming generosity of God's free gifts.

Shin Buddhists find a similar challenge from Amida Buddha, whose generosity is without measure and is not dependent upon human merit. The compassionate vow of Amida Buddha embraces all beings without exception and delivers them from the cycle of striving, competition, and envy. Amida Buddha has a heart of great joy which rejoices in other beings' good fortune and a heart of great giving-up, which reaches out to all beings equally, turning over all his merits to them.

The Japanese Shin Buddhist Shinran (1173–1262) warned that to use religious practices as a form of self-assertion and competition was a great delusion. Shinran suspected that for many people it is extremely difficult to let go of their own striving for a religious reward. He challenged them to let go of their pride and accept enlightenment as a gift freely received. In receiving the gift of Amida Buddha's compassion, we become one with the Buddha and all the universe, and we can genuinely rejoice when others receive gifts they have not earned.

The Zen tradition is also aware that the giving and receiving of gifts has great power to transform human life. Dogen also stressed the significance of giving and its power to overcome the separations between ourselves and others. Where Shinran emphasized receiving a gift without worrying about merit, Dogen stressed the importance of giving as one of the bodhisattva's methods of guidance:

> "Giving" means nongreed. Nongreed means not to covet. Not to covet means not to curry favor. . . . Give your valuables, even a penny or a blade of grass. . . . Moreover, in giving, mind transforms the gift and the gift transforms mind.[36]

The basis for true giving is what Dogen calls "identity-action": "'Identity-action' means nondifference. It is nondifference from self, nondifference from others. . . . When we know identity-action, others and self are one."[37] Genuine giving is the realization that the differences and divisions between ourselves and others are illusory.

John Daido Loori notes that according to
Dogen: "In complete *dana* (giving), there is no separation between the giver and the receiver."[38] Giving is an
act of oneness flowing from our awareness of identity
with others and bringing forth this awareness. Thus
Dogen can claim that the mind transforms the gift and
the gift transforms the mind.

For Shin and Zen Buddhists alike, the heart of
giving and receiving is the overcoming of the false sense
of our own independent existence over against others.
When this happens, there is no cause to worry over
what we deserve or to envy another's good fortune. As
Dogen points out, the greatest valuables we have to give
can be very ordinary objects, "even a penny or a blade
of grass." Valuables and truth become one another in
the process of giving: "The truth can turn into valuables;
valuables can turn into the truth. This is all because the
giver is willing."[39] Giving and receiving are not actions
that we may or may not do without impact on ourselves.
Genuine giving and receiving threaten our ordinary self,
for they destroy the delusion of our separate existence.

In the case of the parable of Jesus, Buddhists
would cut through the workers' complaints just as
firmly, but from a somewhat different perspective.

According to both Shinran and Dogen, genu-
ine giving challenges us to stop thinking of the divisions
among us as ultimately real and to recognize our interdependence. As long as we cling fiercely to the delusion
of our own inherently existing self and our own independent existence, we remain caught in the web of deception. To let go of our self frees us to be able to give and
receive without anxiety and to rejoice in another's good
fortune without worrying about envious comparisons.

☐ *At that time the disciples*
approached Jesus
and said,

> *"Who is the greatest in*
> *the kingdom of heaven?"*

He called a child over,
placed it in their midst,
and said:

> *"Amen I say to you,*
> *unless you turn*
> *and become like children,*
> *you will not enter*
> *the kingdom of heaven."* ☐

(Matthew 18:1–3)

7 Like Little Children

A ZEN STUDENT TRAVELED FOR MILES TO MEET A FAMOUS ZEN TEACHER. WHEN AT LAST HE FOUND him, he asked, "What is the Buddha nature?" In reply, the Zen master asked, "Who are you?" The student had asked the wrong question.

One of the most difficult and important of all arts is the art of asking the right question. A real question reveals a great deal about ourselves, for it implies a whole set of concerns and values. A question implies a judgment on what is worth caring about, what is worth knowing. A real question is never based upon ignorance alone, but on a sense of who we are, a recognition of our limits, a grasp of the situation we face, a sense of what is questionable about ourselves and our world. The art of asking questions cannot be taught, though it can be nurtured and supported or mocked and crushed. An old Buddhist saying tells us that the question is the answer and the answer is the question.

One of the things that is both astonishing and yet reassuring about the disciples of Jesus in the Gospel of Matthew is that they never learn the art of asking the right question. Whenever they take the opportunity to ask Jesus something, they ask the wrong question. By chapter eighteen of the Gospel of Matthew, the disciples have known Jesus for some time. He has already sent them out on a mission of preaching and healing; he has told them about losing themselves to find themselves. Just a few lines earlier, Jesus has told them about his own approaching death.

But almost immediately after learning about Jesus's imminent death, the disciples ask, "Who is the most important in the Kingdom of God?" Their main concern is their own status.

Who is important? Lurking beneath the question of importance is the nagging question of our own identity. The quest for importance is based upon distinguishing ourselves from others, standing out above our competitors. Faced with the news of the death of Jesus, what is most pressing for the disciples is their own self-importance. Rather than entering into Jesus's struggle, they worry about their own advancement.

In reply, Jesus, like the Zen masters who answer a question with a question, does not give a simple answer. Instead, he offers a counter-image which is really a putting in question of the question, a radical attack on the usual way of grounding our identity. Jesus turns to the image of a child, an image which critiques the question of importance and opens up a different way of grounding our identity. The child represents the memory of a time before we grew up and were molded into a world of competing egos and clashing wills. The child represents a dream of lost innocence, a way of living prior to the differentiation of roles in adult life.

Perhaps the heart of the image of the child is the sense of trust, of radical dependence upon God as the foundation of our identity. Since we share this fundamental dependence upon God with every other creature, it relativizes the distinctions we erect between ourselves and others and radically undercuts the questions of rank and power and importance. The image of the child standing before the ambitious disciples is a challenge to let go of the relentless search for importance. The self defined by social, political, educational, and economic roles—the self that we think is so important—can be a delusion.

While Zen Buddhists would not share Jesus's sense of dependence upon God, they also delight in subverting the quest for self-importance. There is a famous legend of the first meeting of Bodhidharma (d. 532), who brought Zen from India to China, with the Emperor Wu of the Liang Dynasty.

> The emperor asked, "Since ascending to the throne, I have had temples built, sutras transcribed, and monks ordained. What merit have I gained?"
>
> The master answered: "No merit at all."
>
> The emperor replied: "Why no merit at all?"
>
> The master said: "All these are but impure motives for merit; they mature the paltry fruit of rebirth as a human being or a deva (a god). They are like shadows that follow the form, having no reality of their own."
>
> The emperor said: "Then of what kind is true merit?"
>
> He answered: "It is pure knowing, wonderful and perfect. Its essence is emptiness. One cannot gain such merit by worldly means."
>
> Thereupon the emperor asked: "What is the sacred truth's first principle?"
>
> The master replied: "Vast emptiness, nothing sacred."

The emperor said: "Who is this who faces me?"
The master replied: "I don't know."[40]

As Jesus challenged the very basis of his disciples' questions of importance, so Bodhidharma challenged the presuppositions of the questions of Emperor Wu. The emperor is asking a series of wrong questions and thus can never find the identity he is seeking. Like the disciples of Jesus who really seek their own importance, the emperor really wants to be praised for the merit he has earned and thus is pursuing the wrong goal. All his actions will only reinforce the power of the delusory self. Bodhidharma, by contrast, makes no claim to an identity based on merit. Awakened to emptiness, he does not even know who he is!

The Buddhist account goes on to say that the emperor was not enlightened after this dialogue. Similarly, the gospel of Matthew tells us that the disciples were not enlightened by Jesus's image of the child—two chapters later they are still fighting over who will be the most important in the kingdom of heaven (20:20–24). Both Jesus and Bodhidharma issue a challenge to decenter the ego, to let go of our concern for self-importance in order to find our true identity. Both have difficulty being understood.

□ *In the beginning was the Word;*
the Word was with God
and the Word was God.

He was in the beginning with God.

All things came to be through him,
and without him nothing came to be.

What came to be through him was life,
and this life
was the light of the human race;

the light shines in the darkness,
and the darkness has not overcome it. . . .

And the Word became flesh,
and made his dwelling among us,
and we saw his glory,
the glory as of the Father's only Son,
full of grace and truth. □

(John 1:1–5, 14)

8 Light in Darkness

BUDDHISM IS FASCINATED BY THE PARADOXICAL INTERPENETRATION, EVEN THE IDENTITY, OF light and darkness. A Zen saying claims: "Light and dark, each at bottom the other."[41] D. T. Suzuki noted that in Buddhist scriptures, "the darkness of the cave itself turns into enlightenment when a torch of spiritual insight burns. . . . [E]nlightenment and darkness are substantially one and the same thing from the very beginning."[42] For Buddhists, light and dark are images of enlightenment and ignorance and also images of the absolute and the relative which are one with each other. To see light in darkness is to realize the meaning of nonduality and to see the Buddha-nature in all things. This is not merely thinking a concept but experiencing the existence of all things as empty.

A Zen monk once asked the Zen master Chao-Chou (778–897) if a dog has Buddha-nature. The Zen master answered, "*Mu* [Nothingness]!" Zenkei

Shibayama, commenting on this exchange, notes that the monk asking the question knew very well that all things have the Buddha-nature. If Chao-Chou had answered either "Yes" or "No," he would be offering a theoretical, conceptual answer which would be wrong. Shibayama observes:

> Although literally "Mu" means No, in this case it points to the incomprehensible satori [enlightenment] which transcends both yes and no, to the religious experience of the Truth one can attain when he casts away his discriminating mind.[43]

What is at stake in the question about the Buddha-nature and the dog is a way of viewing ourselves and all beings, a way of seeing all things in one thing, and each thing in all things. For Buddhists, the absolute is the relative and the relative is the absolute. This is not to be understood simply as a philosophical concept, however. While we can say easily enough that all beings are the Buddha-nature, we can truly grasp this only through direct experience. Properly understood, the question about the Buddha-nature provokes a crisis in our self-understanding, a crisis that is resolved only when our dualistic consciousness is destroyed and our eyes are opened to the nonduality, the transparency of all things.

Shibayama tells us: "We should not read it as an old story; you yourself have to *be* directly 'Mu'. . . . Then the Buddha Nature is 'Mu'; [Chao-Chou] is 'Mu'. Not only that, you yourself and the whole universe are nothing but 'Mu'."[44]

In the Gospel of John the themes of light and darkness confront us with a decision and provoke a crisis in our self-understanding. The hymn that begins the Gospel describes the fundamental rhythm of the cosmos, the arising of all reality through light shining in darkness. All things in the universe are in the divine Word, and the divine Word is in all created things.

The struggle between light and darkness dominates the entire gospel. Jesus describes the judgment of the world as a conflict between them: "the light came into the world, but people preferred darkness to light, because their works were evil" (John 3:19). The light that shines in the darkness is not a theoretical concept but the presence of the power of God in the person of Jesus, a presence which comes as a direct challenge to ordinary human self-understanding.

The central concern of the Gospel of John is the existential encounter with the Word incarnate and the process of learning how to see ourselves and the world in the light of the Word. The rhythms of the cosmos have become the rhythms of the life of Jesus. Thus the narrative of the life of Jesus is the story of the ordering principle of all reality, the key to the meaning of all time and space. For the Gospel of John, to appreciate the meaning of light and darkness will require the entire account of the life, death, and resurrection of Jesus.

The manifestation of the light in Jesus is not a peaceful process, however. The encounter with the incarnate Word provokes a crisis in people's self-understanding and forces them to a decision either for or against the light. For Buddhists, the key to the meaning of the universe is not the narrative of the life of the Buddha but rather the moment of his awakening—his insight into the emptiness and nonduality of all things.

PART II

Oxherds and Shepherds: The Search for the Self

D URING THE SUNG DYNASTY IN CHINA THE ZEN MASTER CHING-CHU USED A SERIES OF DRAW-ings of an ox to illustrate the process of coming to enlightenment. In the series of five pictures the ox became progressively lighter and lighter until the ox completely vanished, representing the realization of emptiness.

Another Zen master, Kuo-an Shih-yuan (ca. 1150), thought that this conclusion was dangerous, for it suggested that vanishing into emptiness was the goal of the Zen life.[45] So Kuo-an drew ten oxherding pictures, each accompanied by a poem. The series became very famous and has been reproduced and redrawn count-less times.

In the first of Kuo-an's scenes, a man is looking for an ox that he has lost. The ox represents the man's own self, which in one sense is not missing at all. It is not at a distance and has never been lost. The man has been deceived and deluded by his own selfish desires, however, and so he wanders about aimlessly, seeking vainly for what is already his.

In the second picture, the man sees the traces of the ox. By hearing Buddhist teaching, he begins to understand that the things around him comprising the objective world are really reflections of the self he is seeking. He does not fully understand what this means, however, and so he continues to wander.

In the third scene, the man sees the ox. He has grasped the meaning of the arising of all things. The fourth scene presents the man catching the ox, but he has difficulty controlling it. The ox is wild and difficult to master, and the man has to use a rope and whip to subdue it.

The fifth scene shows the man herding the ox. Through a fierce program of discipline the ox has been tamed, and now it follows the man willingly without force. In the sixth picture, the man rides the obedient ox home. The struggle has ended. In the seventh picture, the ox has vanished, and the man is alone and serene. There is nothing for him to seek, and he has no more need of his whip or rope.

The eighth scene is an empty circle, representing emptiness. Both the ox and the man have vanished. There is no trace of separation or dualism. There is no search because there is no loss.

The ninth scene portrays a landscape without either the man or the ox. It represents the return to the origin. The man does not appear in the picture, but he observes things without identifying with any illusions. The tenth scene shows the man entering the city "with bliss-bestowing hands." He leaves his isolated and peaceful thatched hut to enter the marketplace, holding a gourd, which represents emptiness. In the city he associates with wine-drinkers and butchers, and all of them together become Buddhas, enlightened beings.

In Zen Buddhism the search for the self is a paradoxical search for a self which we ordinarily do not know but which is not separate from ourselves. The Chinese Zen master Huang-Po (d. 850) explained:

> When you have within yourself a deep insight into this you immediately realize that all that you need is there in perfection, and in abundance, and nothing is at all wanting in you. . . . [W]hen you come to have a realization in one thought, it is no other than this that you are from the first the Buddha himself and no other. The realization has not added anything to you over this truth. . . . Therefore, it is told by the Tathagata [Buddha] that he had nothing attained when he had enlightenment.[46]

In Buddhism, the true self is not separate from ourselves even when we are most deceived by delusions and desires. We search in vain outside for what is our deepest reality. Thus the Heart Sutra says that there is "no knowledge, no attainment, no realization."[47] Zen Buddhism combines a rigid insistence upon discipline with a warning not to pursue enlightenment.

A Buddha does not cling to desires, and so one cannot become a Buddha through desire. Dogen warned: "Have no designs on becoming a Buddha."[48] A twelfth-century Zen poet, Kakua exclaimed: "Satori seekers make me sick!"[49] The undercutting of the desire to be a Buddha and the subversion of any hope of gain do not mean a lax, carefree abandonment of the quest. On the contrary, Zen Buddhism has flourished in countries where strong ascetic discipline was highly valued. The lack of goal and desire is rather a way of being free, even within the most highly disciplined techniques of meditation and practice.

For the Zen Buddhist tradition, we must make our own decisions to change our lives. Zen Buddhists have generally stressed forms of practice such as sitting meditation (Dogen) or meditation on paradoxical sayings or questions called koans (Lin-chi [Japanese: Rinzai]). Zen Buddhists insist that while Shakyamuni Buddha can guide us by his teaching, we ourselves must make the decisive breakthrough to genuine existence and understanding. No one else can accomplish enlightenment for us. No one else can cut through our attachments and entanglements and desires.

There is a very important counterpoint to this teaching in the Shin Buddhist tradition in Japan, which questions the effectiveness of any human resolutions and practice. The Shin tradition invokes the name of the compassionate Amida Buddha and trusts in his gracious vow to save all beings.

The Shin tradition cherishes a story told by Shakyamuni Buddha in the Muryojukyo (Teaching of Infinite Life) Sutra.[50] The story tells of the Bodhisattva Hozo, who was so moved by the sufferings of sentient beings that he resolved to establish a perfect land where all beings could be freed from suffering. He made forty-eight vows, promising to bring all beings to happiness and peace in his perfect land. He vowed not to accept enlightenment if this were not accomplished. Hozo labored for ages and ages until he fulfilled his vows perfectly, achieving such merit that his wisdom and compassion were infinite in space and time. Hozo came to be known as Amida Buddha, the Buddha of Infinite Light and Eternal Life. His accomplishments were made known by Shakyamuni Buddha.

Shin Buddhists refuse to trust their own efforts to attain enlightenment because they caution that even the best efforts to save and enlighten ourselves are never perfect and complete. Such efforts can reinforce a dualistic consciousness that sees ourselves as separate from others. Only through trusting in the compassion of Amida Buddha can we find peace and fulfillment. They express this trust in the *"Nembutsu,"* a brief chant: *namu-amida-butsu,* which literally means "Adoration of the Buddha of Infinite Light."[51] Shinran interpreted the Nembutsu to mean taking refuge in the vow of Amida Buddha to save all beings.[52]

Amida Buddha, however, is not simply a separate figure apart from the person calling his name. D. T. Suzuki notes that "namu-amida-butsu" symbolizes "the unification of Amida and the devotee, wherein the duality no longer exists. This however does not indicate that the devotee is lost or absorbed in Amida so that his individuality is no longer tenable as such. . . . This ambivalence is the mystery of the *Nembutsu.*"[53] Namu-amida-butsu names the fundamental reality—variously called Amida Buddha or emptiness or the Buddha-nature—that is the source of enlightenment. Shin Buddhists chant the Nembutsu as an expression of trust in and gratitude for the vow of Amida Buddha to save all beings.

The paths of Zen and Shin are not as ultimately incompatible as they may seem at first. Suzuki stresses the necessity of uniting the two traditions: "If Zen is the ultra 'self-power' wing of Buddhism, Shin represents the other extreme wing known as the 'other-power', and these two extremes are synthesized in the enlightened Buddha-consciousness."[54] The Japanese philosopher Hajime Tanabe (1885–1962) deliberately draws from both the Zen and the Shin traditions, while also relating the Buddhist experience of salvation to the Christian experience of dying and rising.[55] Tanabe, following the Shin tradition, insists that we cannot enlighten ourselves through our own efforts. We must rely on Other-Power. Other-Power is the power of absolute transformation or conversion.

We experience Other-Power as a gift of sheer grace, often coming at moments of extreme weakness and exhaustion. It is not, however, the action of some other substance or thing upon us. Other-Power is not ultimately other than ourselves, for it overcomes the separation and dichotomy between ourselves and others. Tanabe explains that "what characterizes metanoesis [conversion] is the fact that although it is my own action, at the same time it is not my own action, or conversely, that the absolute transformation that is not my action nonetheless is my action."[56]

Even in Zen Buddhism's path of self-power there is a profound paradox, for there ultimately is no separately existing, individual "self" to rely on. In both the Shin invocation of Amida Buddha and the Zen experience of enlightenment all the distinctions and polarities of the ordinary world disappear, and we realize that we are not other than the universe.

Awakening to our real self means letting go of the delusory ego that dominates our everyday existence. We have in fact been the real self all the time. Other-Power is the power of emptiness or the Buddha-nature; it is not finally separate from self-power. We have always possessed the Buddha-nature, we have always shared in emptiness, even though we have been caught in the web of ignorance which hid us from ourselves.

To express this perspective, Buddhists love to play with seemingly outrageous paradoxes of there being no goal, no gain to the rigorous exercises of meditation. The goal demands extreme discipline and dedication, but it is already present, and so there is no profit to be gained from Buddhist practice. In enlightenment we remain who we are and yet we experience all things anew.

In a rather different sense, the Christian experience of grace can also be understood as a union of Other-Power and self-power. In the Gospel of John, Jesus prays that his followers may "all be one, just as Father, you are in me and I am in you, so that they also may be in us" (17:21). Grace is a gift coming from beyond ourselves, and yet the experience of grace is itself the overcoming of the duality between God and ourselves. Athanasius insisted that the Word "assumed humanity so that we might become God."[57] Augustine knew that we cannot believe in God unless God brings about in us the very will to believe.[58] Augustine also held, following Paul (1 Corinthians 2:11–12), that when we know God's thoughts it is none but the Spirit of God that truly knows them.[59] Nicholas of Cusa suggested that the unnameable God could be named "Not-other."[60] The divinization of the human person in the Christian experience of grace and the awakening of the Buddhist to emptiness are, to be sure, very different experiences. There is in both, nonetheless, an experience of nonduality. To adapt a Zen phrase, in the Christian experience of grace, God and ourselves— "self and Other"—are not two.

□ *What man among you having a hundred sheep*
   and losing one of them
would not leave the ninety-nine in the desert
   and go after the lost one until he finds it?

And when he does find it,
   he sets it on his shoulders with great joy
   and, upon his arrival home,
   he calls together his friends and neighbors
   and says to them,

"Rejoice with me because I have found my lost sheep."

I tell you, in just the same way there will be more
   joy in heaven over one sinner who repents
   than over ninety-nine righteous people
   who have no need of repentance. □

(Luke 15:4–7)

9 A Lost Sheep

TAI-AN OF FU-CHOU ASKED PAI-CHANG, "I WISH TO KNOW ABOUT THE BUDDHA; WHAT IS HE?"

Answered Pai-chang, "It is like seeking for an ox while you are yourself on it."

"What shall I do after I know?"

"It is like going home riding on it."

"How do I look after it all the time in order to be in accordance with [the Dharma]?"

The master then told him, "You should behave like a cowherd, who, carrying a staff, sees to it that his cattle won't wander away into somebody else's rice fields."[61]

Zen master Pai-chang (749–814) proposes a most humorous image: in seeking the Buddha, we are looking for the ox that we are already seated upon. We fail to recognize what is right before us. As a Buddhist proverb says: "Fish do not know of water while they are in water."[62] Thus when we awaken, Pai-chang suggests, it is like a journey home.

Even though the reality we seek is right before us, the Zen tradition insists, nonetheless, that the search for the ox—for the true self that has never been far from us—requires tremendous resolution, persistence, and discipline. The delusory self that blinds us to who we are is extremely well-entrenched in our patterns of thinking and acting, and so the discovery of what is obvious requires rigorous training and constant mindfulness. Pai-chang warns Tai-an that even after discovering the ox on which he is sitting, he must be watchful and take great care that his cattle do not stray—that he does not lose sight of his true self. Awakening is never an achievement to be taken for granted.

The image of Pai-chang recalls the series of oxherding pictures. The oxherd, like Tai-an, begins his quest by looking for what was never distant. He has become so alienated from himself that he does not know who he is. On awakening, he will discover that he and the ox have never been separated.

The Christian tradition also knows of humankind's search for understanding. Jesus encourages his followers to seek: "Ask and it will be given to you; seek and you will find; knock and the door will be opened to you" (Matthew 7:7). Jesus admonishes his followers to badger God in prayer like a persistent widow (Luke 18:1–5) or an importunate friend (Luke 11:5–8), and he praises those who press him for a favor—such as the centurion (Matthew 8:5–13) and the Canaanite woman (Matthew 15:21–28). The prize often comes unexpectedly, however. The parables of the pearl of great price and the treasure buried in a field (Matthew 13:44–46) describe the great joy of the unexpected discovery of the reign of God.

There is a paradoxical twist in the Christian tradition's image of the search. Where the Buddhist tradition chides us for seeking what we already possess, Jesus suggests that the one we are seeking is also seeking us. The search is not just a human endeavor, but a divine quest as well. According to Jesus's parable of the lost sheep, there is a real separation between God and human sinners, but it is God who is searching for lost humans even more fervently than humans are searching for God.

In the Gospel of Luke, Jesus tells the parable of the lost sheep in response to the scribes and Pharisees who disapprove of Jesus's table companions—people known to be disreputable sinners. In reply, Jesus portrays God as a shepherd, a rather startling image in his day. In first-century Palestine, shepherding was regarded as a dishonorable calling, for shepherds were suspected of dishonesty and embezzlement.[63] Even more strange, God does not appear to be a very prudent shepherd. No reasonable shepherd would leave a flock untended in order to search for a single lost sheep. The other sheep could all too easily wander off, and the end result would be worse than before.[64] God appears as a foolish, even reckless member of a despised occupation.

The surprising outcome of this folly is joy: the joy of the shepherd discovering the lost sheep, which offers a glimpse of the joy in heaven over the reconciliation of a lost sinner. Such is Jesus's defense of his own reckless conduct—cavorting with people known to be sinners.

The Buddhist oxherding pictures end on a similar note of almost scandalous surprise. After awakening to his true identity, the oxherd does not retreat into isolation but enters the city where he associates with wine-drinkers and butchers—the people who break the Buddhist precepts not to drink liquor or to kill animals. They are precisely the ones who should be the furthest from enlightenment. The startling conclusion: all are enlightened together. The oxherd "is found in company with wine-bibbers and butchers; he and they are all converted into Buddhas."[65]

For the Buddhist, enlightenment can come as the result of a long and disciplined search by the oxherd and also as a free and surprising gift to those one least expects. In the parables of Jesus, the God we seek is revealed as the one who is recklessly, foolishly seeking us.

☐ *[But] take care not to perform righteous deeds*
in order that people may see them;
    otherwise, you will have no recompense from
    your heavenly Father.

When you give alms,
    do not blow a trumpet before you,
    as the hypocrites do
    in the synagogues and in the streets
    to win the praise of others.

Amen, I say to you,
    they have received their reward. . . .

When you fast,
    do not look gloomy
    like the hypocrites.
    They neglect their appearance,
    so that they may appear to others
    to be fasting.

Amen, I say to you,
    they have received their reward.

But when you fast,
    anoint your head and wash your face,
    so that you may not appear to be fasting,
    except to your Father who is hidden.

And your Father who sees what is hidden
    will repay you. ☐

(Matthew 6:1–2, 16–17)

10 Religious Acts

Before Siddhartha Gautama was enlightened and became Shakyamuni Buddha, he undertook a quest for wisdom. He went to a forest where Indian ascetics did penance. One of the holy men explained to him: "By such penances endured for a time . . . by the path of pain they eventually dwell in happiness—pain, they say, is the root of merit."[66] Siddhartha listened and reflected and rejected this approach. He observed that this type of asceticism was really a sophisticated form of selfishness. The ascetics were punishing themselves in this life so that they could have more pleasure in the next world. Thus, "religion here bears irreligion as its fruit."[67] The ascetics are not really different from sensualists who indulge themselves in this world. The ascetics are just a bit more shrewd.

Jesus gives a similar warning about the practices of fasting and almsgiving. He tells us not to fast so that others can see what we are doing. Such fasting is a form of puffing up our own ego and gets us nowhere. Jesus makes a direct attack on any religious practice intended to make us look good, to advance our own reputation. Even in the act of emptying ourselves in fasting, we must empty ourselves of spiritual pride and egotism.

Jesus does acknowledge that our heavenly Father sees the deeds we do in private and will reward us, and yet this should not be the motivation behind our performing them. A Buddhist would question Jesus's assurance of reward if it is taken as the motivation for religious actions. Even if we are trying to impress God by praying alone in our room, we are still seeking a reward and thus, from a Buddhist perspective, not yet truly religious.

Buddhist practice presents a similar paradox. Buddhists do acknowledge benefits from meditation, but insist that as long as we are trying to gain some benefit from the practice, we are not truly meditating. Similarly, Buddhists warn against seeking enlightenment. For if we are seeking enlightenment, we will never find it: we are still seeking to enhance our own separate self, and we have not really let go of our ego at all.

For Buddhists, it is only by letting go of any desire for a reward or self-conscious spiritual advancement of any type that we can be truly religious. In some ways the Buddhist perspective comes close to that of the Book of Job, where God allows Job to be tested to see if he is serving God only for a reward. The Buddhist tradition, not unlike the Book of Job, challenges the truly religious person to let go of any demand to be repaid.

☐ *Then God delivered all these commandments:*

"*I, the LORD, am your God,
who brought you out of the land of Egypt,
that place of slavery.*

You shall not have other gods besides me.

*You shall not carve idols for yourselves
in the shape of anything in the sky above
or on the earth below
or in the waters beneath the earth;*

*you shall not bow down before them
or worship them.*" ☐

(Exodus 20:1–5)

11 Commandments

I N BUDDHISM THE QUEST FOR WISDOM LEADS TO INSIGHT INTO THE EMPTINESS OF ALL THINGS. The path to enlightenment is marked by a series of commandments, several of which are identical to the biblical Ten Commandments. The five precepts of the Buddha teach us not to kill, not to steal, not to indulge in sexual excess, not to lie, and not to cloud our consciousness through intoxicants or drugs. The precepts are beginning steps along the way, but their ultimate fulfillment is based upon insight into emptiness.

The cornerstone of the Ten Commandments is that no image is to take the place of God. No thing in the heavens, on the earth, or under the earth is to be worshipped as a resemblance of God. The first commandment is a radical undercutting of any fashioning of an image of God.

In obedience to this command the temple of Jerusalem had no statue of the God of Israel. The ark of the covenant was merely the throne or the footstool of God. God's presence was symbolized by the empty space above the ark. After the first temple was destroyed by the Babylonians and the ark of the covenant was lost, the second temple was rebuilt with the Holy of Holies, the most sacred place on earth, completely empty.[68] In the emptiness of space, the people of Israel honored the presence of God.

The Ten Commandments are really expansions of one command: "There is one God. You shall not carve idols." Idols are ways we fill the void that we fear. We do not want to face the emptiness of the experience of God or of ourselves, and so we turn to other gods. When Moses stayed too long atop the mountain, the people told Aaron to build a god they could see; so they began to build a golden calf that would promise to fill the void (Exodus 32:1-6).

The specific commandments that follow the first are warnings about false ways of filling up our lives. The Sabbath, the summit of creation, is an emptying of time. No work is to be done, for the day belongs to God alone. In the emptiness of time, in ceasing from work, we experience and honor God.

What follows from abandoning all images of God is a respect for others, for life. The commandments lead from the relinquishing of all images of God to a warning against being dominated by desire. In our coveting, we make ourselves the center of our world, and so we desire to abuse things and people. Carving idols and coveting other people and things go together. In emptiness we find healing and wholeness. In the emptiness of space we find the presence of God; in the emptiness of time we find the proper reverence for God.

In Buddhism the three poisons of human life are greed, anger, and ignorance. As long as we cling to the delusion of possessing a separate, inherently existing self, these dominate our lives. Once the self is forgotten and emptiness is realized, however, the three poisons are transformed into compassion, wisdom, and realization.

While Buddhists do not have a polemic against idolatry, they do reject any definition, any limitation of emptiness or the Buddha-nature. Even the image of the Buddha is not to be clung to. One time a monk asked Ma-tsu (709–788), "What is Buddha?" Ma-tsu replied, "No mind, no Buddha."[69] The answer was especially jarring because in an earlier encounter, Ma-tsu had been asked the exact same question and had answered, "Mind is Buddha." By using two directly contradictory answers Ma-tsu undercuts any conceptual interpretation and offers an invitation to let go of attachment to any name and form, including that of the Buddha. What is needed to realize emptiness is not a concept but direct experience. As Shibayama expresses the challenge of Ma-tsu: "[D]on't be dragged around by his words; leap out of the expressions! Then for the first time you will be a truly free man."[70]

☐ *Then Jesus spoke to the crowds*
and to his disciples,
saying,

> *"The scribes and the Pharisees have taken*
> *their seat on the chair of Moses.*
> *Therefore, do and observe all things*
> *whatsoever they tell you,*
> *but do not follow their example.*
> *For they preach but they do not practice. . . .*
>
> *All their works are performed to be seen.*
> *They widen their phylacteries*
> *and lengthen their tassels.*
> *They love places of honor at banquets,*
> *seats of honor in synagogues,*
> *greetings in marketplaces,*
> *and the salutation, 'Rabbi'. . . .*
>
> *The greatest among you*
> *must be your servant."* ☐

(Matthew 23:1–3, 5–7, 11)

12 Self and Religion

 OGEN WARNED HIS STUDENTS:

If you worry about how others will react to your
words and deportment, if you refrain from doing
certain things because others will consider
them bad, or if you do good thinking that others
will admire you for it as a Buddhist, you still
cling to the conditioned world. . . . Be aware of
each thing as it arises.[71]

Jesus raises the question: What is religion all
about? Is religion basically a form of morality, a set of
things to do so we can get a reward from God, a set of
rules to follow? If so, religion can be a very subtle form of
self-seeking, based upon the belief: If I do this, God will
owe me something.

Jesus is attacking not just blatant hypocrisy of
the self-righteous but the whole attitude that religion is
primarily a set of rules to be observed for a reward. For

Jesus, being religious is not a matter of being very good so that God will grant a reward but rather a response to the inbreaking of the reign of God. The heart of being religious is not morality but grace.

Buddhists warn us, "Holiness stinks!" The attempt to use a system of religious practice to separate or elevate oneself above others is to remain in ignorance and illusion. In the eighth of the oxherding pictures, in the realization of emptiness, "even the idea of holiness does not obtain. He does not linger about where the Buddha is, and as to where there is no Buddha he speedily passes by. . . . A holiness before which birds offer flowers is but a farce."[72]

Buddhists radically undercut the use of religion to advance one's ego. For the Buddhist, I am not a substantial thing or a being that endures through time; I am a series of events, a constant coming-to-be. For Buddhists, the great tragedy of human existence comes from ignorance of our true condition and clinging to illusions, clinging to our own petty egos. To do this in a religious way can be especially pernicious because it can be so subtle and self-deceiving. This causes suffering both for ourselves and others.

A fifteenth-century Japanese Buddhist imagined a skeleton telling him: "Give up the idea 'I exist.' Just let your body be blown along by the wind of the floating clouds; rely on this."[73]

For Buddhists, the goal of religious practice is to realize emptiness, to empty ourselves of our clinging to our delusory self. To be empty means to be open to what is there, to whatever may be. One then is perfectly full. To realize emptiness does not result in indifference, but brings true compassion. In letting go we find wisdom and compassion.

☐ *[But] what ever gains I had,*
   these I have come to consider a loss
   because of Christ.

   More than that,
   I even consider everything as a loss
   because of the supreme good of knowing
   Christ Jesus my Lord.

For his sake
I have accepted the loss of all things
and I consider them so much rubbish,

   that I may gain Christ
   and be found in him,
   not having any righteousness of my own
   based on the law
   but that which comes through faith in Christ,

the righteousness from God
depending on faith. . . . ☐

(Philippians 3:7–9)

13 Loss, Gain, and Grace

P AUL CLAIMS TO HAVE BEEN ONE OF THE BEST AT KEEPING THE LAW. IN LIGHT OF HIS EXPERIENCE of Christ, however, he accounts the whole system of trying of achieve salvation through following rules as rubbish. He finds that adherence to the law is not the true way of living and risks becoming a self-centered way of gaining approval. Paul warns us that we are all caught in sin and all dependent upon the offer of God's grace.

For Paul the experience of sin destroys the illusion that we can master our own destiny, solve our own dilemmas without the grace and love of God.

One side of Buddhist teaching seems to run directly contrary to Paul's insistence on grace. Buddhists often warn that no one else can save us, no one else can purify our consciousness. However, Mahayana Buddhists also know that the ego can in no way save itself. The Indian philosopher Nagarjuna (ca. 150–200) insisted that the ego will not destroy itself, and therefore cannot free itself from illusion. The harder it tries, the more it binds itself in desire and deception.

Centuries later, Shinran had an experience very similar to Paul's. He concluded that however good we may be, we are unable to achieve our own rebirth in the Pure Land of Amida Buddha. If even good persons are unable, "bad persons" are all the more unable. Amida Buddha, however, has taken a vow to save us because of his great love. If we trust in his compassion to the end, we will be saved. Shinran concluded with the paradox: "Even a good person attains birth in the Pure Land, how much more so the evil person."[74] He went on to explain:

> The reason is that since the person of self-power, being conscious of doing good, lacks the thought of entrusting himself completely to Other Power, he is not the focus of the Primal Vow of Amida [Buddha]. But when he turns over self-power and entrusts himself to Other Power, he attains birth in the land of True Fulfillment.[75]

Letting go of self means letting go even of our desire to save ourselves, perhaps the hardest release of all.

□ *[Y]et I live,*

   no longer I,

   but Christ lives in me; . . . □

(Galatians 2:20)

14 Not with My Own Life

T HE JAPANESE ZEN BUDDHIST PHILOSOPHER KEIJI NISHITANI INTERPRETS THIS SAYING OF PAUL AS a "Christian koan," and poses the question: "That makes sense to me immediately. Allow me only to ask you this: Who is speaking here?"[76] Who says this statement? If the "I" who speaks no longer lives, who makes the claim?

The linguistic expression of Zen Buddhist experience often takes the form of a koan, a paradoxical problem or question that a student is challenged to resolve. A Zen master once explained the role of a koan in Zen training: "The koan . . . throws a student into a steep and rugged maze where he has no sense of direction at all. He is expected to overcome all the difficulties and find the way out himself."[77]

A good koan is deliberately disorienting, baffling, disabling. "In short, the role of the koan is not to lead us to satori easily, but on the contrary to make us lose our way and drive us to despair."[78]

There is both in the Zen koan and in the letters of Paul a combination of a fierce commitment to discipline and a radical letting go of reliance on one's own powers, a search for one's true identity and an experience of the death of one's self.

Paul repeatedly attacks the sense of self-sufficiency. Zen throws students upon their own resources, but also challenges them to realize that they have no-self. For both Paul and Zen, the experience of transformation is an overcoming of the separation between self and Other. Paul also wrote:

> [W]e do not know how to pray as we ought, but the Spirit itself intercedes with inexpressible groanings. And the one who searches hearts knows what is the intention of the Spirit, because it intercedes for the holy ones according to God's will (Romans 8:26–27).

We may wonder, in the spirit of Nishitani's question: When it is the Spirit who prays in me to God, who is praying here?

☐ *Along the way [Jesus] asked his disciples,*
"Who do people say that I am?"

> *They said in reply,*
> *"John the Baptist,*
> *others Elijah,*
> *still others one of the prophets."*

And he asked them,
"But who do you say that I am?"

> *Peter said to him in reply,*
> *"You are the Messiah."*

Then he warned them not to tell anyone about him.

He began to teach them
> *that the Son of Man must suffer greatly*
> *and be rejected by the elders,*
> *the chief priests, and the scribes,*
> *and be killed,*
> *and rise after three days. . . .*

He summoned the crowd with his disciples
and said to them,
> *"Whoever wishes to come after me*
> *must deny himself,*
> *take up his cross, and follow me.*

For whoever wishes to save his life
will lose it,
but whoever loses his life
for my sake and that of the gospel
will save it." ☐

(Mark 8:27–31, 34–35)

15 A Question of Identity

D. T. Suzuki warns us that "we are in fact all groping for ourselves, we are like the man who dreamed he had no head of his own and spent all night searching for it outside himself."[79]

Jesus's question about his identity has echoed through the centuries. There are two ways to approach the question. The first is to approach Jesus as an external object of study, possibly as an historical figure of the past or as a special divine being beyond the world of our experience, someone we read about and speculate about, but someone we keep safely at arm's length. In this approach to Jesus we can come out of curiosity. We know who we are and have ourselves together. We do not really want to be changed by the question.

The other way to approach the question is more dangerous and more unsettling. The second way is to see that I can only answer the question about Jesus by relating it to two other questions: "Who is God?" and

"Who am I?" All three questions imply each other, for to ask about Jesus is to ask about oneself and about God.

In acclaiming Jesus as the Messiah, the Christ, the Son of the Living God, Peter is really acknowledging Jesus as the link between our knowledge of ourselves and our knowledge of God. Jesus is the one who reveals who God is and who we are.

What Jesus reveals is that the reality of God is love, but it is a frightening love, for Jesus links his identity as the Messiah to the inevitability of his suffering and death. He himself is to be put to death, and he goes on to warn his followers that they must expect the same. The discovery of Jesus's identity is inextricably linked to the knowledge of his self-sacrifice, and the decision to follow on Jesus's path is an acceptance of the loss of one's self.

In Buddhist dialogues the question of the self is at the heart of the search for wisdom and compassion. The Zen masters repeatedly ask about our true identity, often phrased as a question about "the face we had before we were born." In Buddhism our true self is no-self, our true mind is no-mind. Buddhist teachers never tire of playfully subverting any claim of a self. As long as we believe we have a separate, independent self, our ego is filled with self-seeking, illusory desires, and we are far from enlightenment.

Buddhist monks who ask their teachers about the Buddha are often directed to discover themselves. Insight comes not from speculation or from information about an external figure but from looking into one's self. The Chinese Zen master Lin-chi (ca. 810–866) told his students to seek the truth not in the Buddhas and patriarchs of the past but in the present moment:

> Students today can't get anywhere: what ails you? Lack of faith in yourself is what ails you. . . . Bring to rest the

thoughts of the ceaselessly seeking mind and you'll not differ from the Patriarch-Buddha. Do you want to know the Patriarch-Buddha? He is none other than you who stand before me listening to my discourse.[80]

Buddhist enlightenment, like the Christian's discovery of the identity of Jesus as the Christ, cannot be understood or attained through detached, curious speculation. It involves a radical transformation of our way of being and relating. To understand who Christ is, who the Buddha is, and who we are, is to lose ourselves. This loss is both our transformation and our fulfillment.

☐ *Then the scribes and the Pharisees
brought a woman who had been caught in adultery
and made her stand in the middle.*

They said to him,

> *"Teacher, this woman was caught in the very act
> of committing adultery.
> Now in the law,
> Moses commanded us to stone such women.
> So what do you say?" . . .*

*Jesus bent down and began to write on the ground
with his finger.*

*But when they continued asking him,
he straightened up and said to them,*

> *"Let the one among you who is without sin
> be the first to throw a stone at her."*

*Again he bent down and wrote on the ground.
And in response, they went away one by one,
beginning with the elders.*

*So he was left alone with the woman before him.
Then Jesus straightened up and said to her,*

> *"Woman, where are they?
> Has no one condemned you?"* ☐

(John 8:3–5, 6–10)

16 The Judgment

T HE THERAVADA TRADITION OF BUDDHISM TELLS THE STORY OF A SOMEWHAT SIMILAR ENCOUNTER of the young Prince Siddhartha Gautama before he left his palace and family to seek enlightenment:

> A crowd of people were shouting abuse and throwing rocks and sticks at a woman who appeared almost naked. [Siddhartha] hurried up to the scene, and when the people saw him and recognized him, they all retreated and some ran away. A few remained behind. The woman's clothing was dirty and torn into pieces. She could barely hide her nakedness. . . . She was hurt by the darts thrown at her by the people. Blood was flowing from wounds on her head. Siddhartha was furious.
>
> "What has this woman done to be harrassed like this?" he questioned those who remained.
>
> "Sir, she goes around the city half-naked and with disheveled hair, muttering all sorts of unintelligible things. It has become impossible for a young girl or a boy to walk on the street. She is a mad woman. We are trying to drive her away from the streets."
>
> "Has any one of you tried to find out why she has gone mad? Have you tried to help her in any way?"

"No Sir," replied one of the men.
"Don't you feel ashamed of yourself?" asked Siddartha, his
anger rising. "What if it was your mother or sister or a
relative? Would you treat them the same way you do this
woman?"
The few who were present could not look Siddhartha in his
face.[81]

While the similarities between the two stories
are striking, the divergences indicate very different
understandings of the central problem of human existence. Jesus encounters a woman who has sinned and
he forgives her. Siddhartha encounters a woman who is
insane because she has suffered too much and has
withdrawn from reality. On questioning the woman,
Siddhartha learned that while she was expecting her
second child, her husband was bitten by a snake and
died, and then her two-year-old son was snatched off by
a vulture. Her second child died before birth. The
woman was not able to endure the pain and wondered,
"But why should all these things happen to me only?"

In response, Siddhartha tried to awaken the
woman to the universal nature of impermanence and
death. He invited the woman to come to his father's
palace in one week's time, demanding: "But when
you come, you must bring with you a handful of rice
from a house in Kapilavatthu where no death has taken
place."[82] The strategies of the two religious leaders are
characteristically different: where Jesus forgives a sinful
woman, Siddhartha calls a madwoman to awaken to
reality and accept it.

The problem of human existence is expressed
in very different terms by the two stories: the Christian
story is concerned with sin, the Buddhist story with
ignorance—a loss of touch with reality that amounts to
madness.

Both stories agree in also presenting the problem of an angry crowd that delights in tormenting a woman who has broken social norms. In both cases the vengeful crowd only multiplies the harm done. Jesus elsewhere sternly warns his followers: "Stop judging, that you may not be judged. For as you judge, so will you be judged, and the measure with which you measure will be measured out to you" (Matthew 7:1-2).

The Buddhist tradition has a very similar perspective on judging others. In Buddhism to be preoccupied with another person's failings is to defile our own consciousness. The evils we deplore in others we make present in ourselves, and the self-righteous condemnation we pronounce upon others is itself a judgment upon ourselves.

From a Buddhist perspective, wisdom and compassion preclude such condemnations of others. We can only put an end to our own defilements. The attempt to appoint ourselves as judges over others only traps us in a web of self-deception and delusion. While Buddhists have a strict moral code, which prohibits adultery as strongly as the Bible, they would agree with Jesus that the condemnation of another person's sin is not our concern.

The danger that appears when we hear of someone sinning scandalously or behaving eccentrically is the strange fascination in knowing someone else has done wrong. The greater the sin or the eccentricity, the greater the fascination. It may be reassuring to think that we are not as bad or as strange as someone else, but the self-righteous fascination with another's faults is itself really a form of selfishness.

The judgment we pronounce on others is often not an expression of genuine concern for moral values or for the individual involved, but rather an attempt to flee from our own situation. An old Zen saying cautions us:

> One who walks the Way
> Sees not any faults in the world.
> Seeing others' faults
> Means that one's own faults are strengthened.[83]

☐ *Therefore, that I might not become too elated,*
a thorn in the flesh was given to me,
an angel of Satan to beat me,
to keep me from being too elated.

Three times I begged the Lord about this,
that it might leave me,
but he said to me,

"My grace is sufficient for you,
for power is made perfect in weakness."

I will rather boast most gladly of my weaknesses,
in order that the power of Christ
may dwell with me.

Therefore, I am content with weaknesses,
insults, hardships,
persecution, and constraints,
for the sake of Christ;

for when I am weak,
then I am strong. ☐

(2 Corinthians 12:7–10)

17 Other-Power

D|URING NOVEMBER AND DECEMBER OF 1944, AS
THE TIDE OF WORLD WAR II WAS TURNING EVER
more strongly against Japan, Hajime Tanabe gave a
series of lectures at Kyoto University. Tanabe was one of
the most respected religious thinkers in Japan, and the
lecture hall was filled to capacity. Tanabe began his
remarks by saying, "The people of Japan watch in alarm
as their nation sinks deeper and deeper into hell."[84]

Tanabe openly confessed his sense of failure
as a philosopher, as a citizen of Japan, as a human
being. He felt that he shared in the collective responsibility for the state of the Japanese people. He recognized that he should bring his philosophical training to
the aid of the Japanese nation, and yet he felt powerless
to speak out. Torn by indecision, he reached a point of
despair and was ready to abandon his career as a
religious philosopher. At that moment he had an experi-

ence of *metanoesis* or conversion (*zange*), which he called an experience of Other-Power.

When he could no longer do anything on his own power, he experienced Other-Power accepting him with compassion and transforming him. For Tanabe, this experience of conversion is an act of self-surrender, a moment of letting go of our attempt to save ourselves through self-power. It is a paradoxical act: "although it is my own action, at the same time it is not my own action."[85]

From this point on, he developed his thought as "a philosophy achieved through a death-and-resurrection process of transformation."[86] He rediscovered the writings of Shinran and his proclamation of the compassion of Amida Buddha. Tanabe incorporated the experience of conversion and the trust in Amida's compassionate love into the heart of his own self-understanding and his philosophy.

The apostle Paul went through a somewhat similar experience of his own inability to change himself through his own power. Paul had a powerful conversion experience, renounced sin, accepted grace through Jesus Christ, and began to live a transformed life. Yet twenty years after the great turning point in his life, Paul is still wrestling with his own weakness, still caught, trapped in a struggle against himself that he cannot win.

Paul laments that "a thorn in the flesh was given to me, an angel of Satan to beat me, to keep me from being too elated." What was the thorn in the flesh? Was it physical suffering? An angry temper that Paul could not control? A moral failing? No one really knows.

A bishop in the north of Africa in the late fourth and early fifth centuries gave one of the most powerful interpretations of Paul. Augustine, like Paul, examined his own will and decided that in one sense he was free to choose, but in a deeper sense he was not free on his own. He was bound by compulsive urges and irreversible patterns of behavior, the cumulative force of habit. The pleasure of one sin was amplified and transformed in his memory, and then was repeated until he had forged a chain for himself that he was powerless to break.

Augustine found, like Paul and not unlike Tanabe, a persistent tension within himself that continued throughout his life. According to Augustine, the struggle passes through four phases. First, we are in ignorance; we do not even admit our sinfulness to ourselves. We blind ourselves to our own faults and tell ourselves everything is all right.

Secondly, we come to the realization of how lost, how trapped we are, and we experience utter helplessness. Thirdly, we throw ourselves onto a power greater than ourselves, upon the grace offered through a Liberator, through Christ. We trust the words that Paul heard, "My grace is enough for you." But even our power to believe itself comes from God. In this world, Augustine noted, we constantly move back and forth among these three stages. The final stage, of being in peace, is reached only after this life is ended, when the tension is resolved and we enter a definitive state of healing and peace.

For Tanabe, as for Augustine and Paul, we can only change our lives and our wills through a power which is beyond us but somehow one with us. As Tanabe expressed his experience:

> Indeed, I have to admit that even the self-power implied in my practice of *zange* is itself already mediated by Other-power. . . . Self-power and Other-power converge here

and thus penetrate each other. . . . All I can do is submit myself to "naturalness" . . . and let the absolute do as it will.[87]

☐ *Jesus said to him in reply,*

    "What do you want me to do for you?"

The blind man replied to him,

    "Master, I want to see." ☐

(Mark 10:51)

18 Seeing

O NE WORD FOR THE GOAL OF DISCIPLINE AND MEDITATION PRACTICE IN ZEN BUDDHISM IS *kensho,* which means "seeing real." In both Christianity and Buddhism "seeing real" is one of the most difficult and important tasks of human life.

The Zen Master Lin-chi described our true self as "a real man of no titles": "In the naked flesh-mass exists a real man of no titles. He is always coming in and out through your sense-organs. If you don't know him yet, look! look!"

In the Gospel of Mark, a blind man asks to see, and he sees. The story immediately before this passage tells of James and John seeking the best places of glory in the reign of God. The apostles ask for glory because they are blind; they do not see who Jesus really is or what the reign of God really means.

Mark places these two stories back to back to prod us to face the question of whether we can see. Are we so busy looking for something, a future dream of glory or success or power, that we cannot see the person in front of us?

It is so easy to spend huge amounts of time and energy and resources looking for something that we think we lack: happiness, meaning, love, fulfillment, God. We can go all over searching and searching for what is not present and never take the time to see the present moment.

It is so easy to live in the past or the future—in some past regret or hurt, in some future fantasy or fear—that we do not take the time to see what is right before us in the present. Even in our searching for God we often think too much, reflect too much, talk too much, and fail to be attentive to the reality of God in the present moment. We live immersed in God's love like a fish in the ocean.

Buddhists stress both the importance and the difficulty of seeing the present moment. In Buddhism being filled up and preoccupied with our own self prevents us from true seeing, from meeting other people, from experiencing them as they are. The Emperor Wu lamented the failure of his encounter with Bodhidharma, the first Zen patriarch of China: "Alas, seeing, I saw him not; meeting, I met him not. Now I repent and bemoan it as much as I did then." For Buddhists, it is only through the experience of emptiness that we can live in the present and genuinely encounter other persons.

For Buddhists, ultimate reality is right here, all around us. Buddhists warn against seeking some other fulfillment in the future or in another world. In Mahayana Buddhism, the passing, relative world all around us is nirvana, the home of our ultimate fulfillment and peace. The request of the blind man expresses one central challenge of human existence, to see the wonder of the present moment. As the German theologian Friedrich Schleiermacher put it, "Miracle is the religious name for event."

☐ *[The younger son] said to [his father],*

> *"Father, I have sinned against heaven*
> *and against you;*
> *I no longer deserve to be called your son."*

But his father ordered his servants,

> *"Quickly bring the finest robe and put it on him;*
> *put a ring on his finger and sandals on his feet.*
> *Take the fattened calf and slaughter it.*
> *Then let us celebrate with a feast,*
> *because this son of mine*
> *was dead and has come to life again. . . ."*

[The older son] said to his father . . . ,

> *"Look, all these years I served you*
> *and not once did I disobey your orders;*
> *yet you never gave me even a young goat*
> *to feast on with my friends.*
> *But when your son returns who swallowed up*
> *your property with prostitutes,*
> *for him you slaughter the fattened calf."*

He said to him,

> *"My son, you are here with me always;*
> *everything I have is yours.*
> *But now we must celebrate and rejoice,*
> *because your brother was dead*
> *and has come to life again.*
> *He was lost and has been found."* ☐

(Luke 15:21–24, 29–32)

19 Two Sons

T HE BUDDHIST TRADITION ALSO TELLS A STORY OF AN IMPOVERISHED, LOST SON WHO RETURNS to find a wealthy father. While the outward similarities between the Christian and Buddhist stories are striking, the differences may be even more revealing of the concerns of the two traditions.

According to the Buddhist story, an ignorant youth ran away from his father's home and went to another country to live. While they were separated, the son remained poor and the father grew increasingly prosperous. The father meanwhile moved to another city, settling in a magnificent home. Decade after decade the poor son continued to wander from town to town, seeking food and clothing until finally, many years later, he came to the city where his father dwelt.

The father had never ceased to yearn for the day when he could see his son again. He would reflect: "If I could only get [back] my son and commit my wealth to him, how contented and happy should I be, with never any more anxiety!"[88] The son arrived at his father's house and saw him from a distance, seated on a lion couch, wearing priceless pearls and surrounded by important people as well as attendants and slaves.

The son, however, had no idea who the rich man was, and he feared that he would be seized and forced to do hard labor. So he hastened away from the rich man's home.

The father, on the other hand, had recognized his son at once, and sent servants to bring him back. The frightened son refused, and so the servants seized him and dragged him back by force. The young man was so terrified that he fainted. The father saw this from a distance and revived his son with cold water, but then determined to tell no one of their true relationship. Instead, he released the young man.

The father decided to use what Buddhists call a skilful means to establish a relationship with his son. He ordered two other men in the town to hire the wandering beggar, offering him double wages to clear away garbage from the rich man's house. The son accepted the offer, moved into a humble hut, and began to work.

Every day the rich man would watch his son clearing away garbage, and he was filled with compassion. He would disguise himself, putting on dirty clothes, and would approach his son, encouraging him and befriending him. He told the poor young man to look upon him as a father: "Be at ease in your mind; I am as it were your father; do not be worried again."[89] The father gave his son a new name, but the son continued to regard himself as a humble laborer.

Because of his son's low self-understanding, the father employed him in this way for twenty years, having him clear away dirt and garbage. During this time, the younger man came to have confidence in himself and his father, but continued to live in the same place. The father decided to increase his son's position and advance him gradually in rank and responsibility. The father had his son learn the financial details of the granaries and treasuries that the father possessed. The son fulfilled all his responsibilities with honesty, but continued to live in the simple hut and regard himself as a lowly servant.

Finally, the old man felt that he was close to death. He called his son to him and told him: "I need someone upon whom I can bestow my wealth as a deposit, and you must accept it. From now on you are just as much its owner as I am, but you must not squander it."[90]

The poor man accepted the offer, still unaware of his father's identity, but he cared nothing for his new-found wealth and continued to live in his straw hut and do his usual work. Now the father knew that his son would not abuse his inheritance, and so he called his son again, and in front of the king and the people of the town and countryside the old man proclaimed: "This is my son, whom I begot. . . . To him I leave all my family revenues, and my private wealth he shall have as his own."[91]

The Lotus Sutra explains the story: "The very rich elder is the Tathagata [the Buddha] and we all are as the Buddha's sons."[92] The father represents the heavenly Buddha who knows all beings have the Buddha-nature and who has compassion on them. We, however, do not know our own true identity, and thus are afraid of the message of the Buddha when we hear it. We are like the son who does not know his own father, who lives in poverty and misery even though he is heir to a great fortune. To overcome our ignorance, the Buddha adopts skilful means: adapting his message to our capacity, disguising himself in different forms to approach us, and sending bodhisattvas to communicate with us.

Where the Christian story describes a sudden repentance for sin and an immediate celebration of reconciliation, the father in the Buddhist story must make a long detour, disguising himself and putting his son through a long trial before finally sharing his wealth and revealing his identity. The Buddhist story does not believe that too sudden a transformation is possible. The path to enlightenment is gradual and requires patient practice to clear away the dirt and garbage that becloud our awareness. Even though the Buddha may offer us heavenly wealth, we are too deeply deceived by long patterns of thought and action to awaken at once to our true identity.

The awakening of the son and the death of the father may be seen as the climax of the Buddhist process of enlightenment. When awakened to their true identity, Buddhists realize that the Buddha is not other than themselves and that they have possessed the full treasure of enlightenment, the Buddha-nature, all the time. One commentator noted the significance of the death of the father: in awakening, the Buddhist "finds that the heavenly Buddha has ceased to exist for him, that nothing is truly real but the great Emptiness which is peace and Nirvana."[93]

In the Christian story themes of emptiness and fullness also dominate the narrative, but the moments of reversal are more sudden and more dramatic. The younger son wants to be filled with all the "good things" of life, with money and beautiful women.

His path is not unlike the consumer mentality of our society. If something is wrong, we are urged to spend some money to buy something, do something, go somewhere, and we are promised that we will feel better. Above all, we are warned, do not be empty, because then we will be a "nobody" and that would be terrible.

All the time the younger son has money, he is going further and further away from his father, from happiness, from himself. He ends his reckless pursuit of good things with nothing. Jesus describes him as finally "coming to his senses" (15:17). The Greek text literally means "returning to himself."

The strange paradox of the younger son is that when he is full, he is losing himself. When he is empty, when he has lost his money, his friends, even his food, when his stomach is literally an empty space inside of him, then he comes to himself again.

He repents and returns to his father empty, seeking nothing but to be a hired servant. He seeks no money, no friendship, no welcome. Unlike the son in the Buddhist tale, the prodigal son in the parable knows who his father is, but knows also that he is estranged from his father and has no claim upon him.

The father, for his part, is also empty, for he has lost his son and half of his property. Even more important, the father is empty of anger, of the desire to say, "I told you so." He is empty of the urge to scold, empty—in effect—of his own ego. The father is empty and waiting for his son's return. Precisely because both the father and the son are empty, they can embrace each other and find each other.

The older son, on the other hand, is all too full. He owns all that is left of his father's property. He has filled his days with dutiful work and obedient service.

He has filled his heart with resentment. There is no indication that he ever missed his brother or longed for his return. He even refuses to acknowledge his own relationship to his brother, calling him "your son." The older brother's world is full; and when the younger brother returns, there is no place for him.

Precisely because the older brother is filled with goods, with resentments, with himself, he is excluded from the feast. He is left outside complaining while everyone else is inside rejoicing. Because he is always there, he is not really there at all when his brother returns.

If the example of the father is a clue to the way God relates to us, then the key to the Christian's salvation is the emptiness of God. It is precisely because God is not filled up with revenge and anger that God is eager to welcome us home. Because God is like the father in the story, empty and open and yearning for our return, we can turn to God and find a welcome.

The turning point of the Buddhist story is the young man's patient work over many years, a labor which culminates in awakening to the awareness of who he has been all the time. The theme of repentance, which is so central to the parable of Jesus, is pointedly absent from the Buddhist account. The heart of the religious quest for the Buddhist is not repentance for sin, but letting go of a false consciousness and awakening to our true identity. In both stories the son had to be empty of himself in order to learn who he truly was.

A Zen story tells of a professor filled with knowledge who asked a Zen master about the Buddha-nature. The Zen master responded by filling the professor's cup until it overflowed, signifying that he was too full to receive an answer.

□ *In [those] days before the flood,*
[people] were eating and drinking,
marrying and giving in marriage,
up to the day that Noah entered the ark.

> *They did not know until the flood came*
> *and carried them all away.*

So will it be [also]
> *at the coming of the Son of Man. . . .*

Therefore, stay awake!
For you do not know on which day
your Lord will come.

Be sure of this:

> *if the master of the house had known*
> *the hour of night*
> *when the thief was coming,*
> *he would have stayed awake*
> *and not let his house be broken into.*

So too,

> *you also must be prepared,*
> *for at an hour you do not expect,*
> *the Son of Man will come.* □

(Matthew 24:38–39, 42–44)

20 Awakening

A BUDDHIST CHANT WARNS US, "MAY I RESPECTFULLY REMIND YOU, LIFE AND DEATH ARE of supreme importance. . . . Awaken, awaken. Do not squander your life!"

Dogen instructed his students: "If you can spur and arouse your determination with the thought that you might die tonight or tomorrow or that at any time you might meet with some terrible misfortune, you can expect to gain enlightenment."[94]

The days of our lives slip by one into the other in a seemingly endless flow. The passage of time seems continuous, relentless, unending. After a while, the smooth and even flow of time, the repeated rhythm of the same patterns, can seem lulling.

Yet there is always the possibility of an interruption of time, of some event that will break into the onward flow of time and overturn our awareness of ourselves. It has been said that it concentrates the mind wonderfully to know that one will be hanged at sunrise. This rather macabre image catches something of the uneasy urgency of Jesus's warnings about the Son of Man or the Buddhist chant's urgent advice.

"Stay awake . . . be watchful . . . know the time." The language of Jesus is meant to grab our attention, to interrupt the lulling flow of time in a way so forceful that we cannot avoid the urgency of the moment. The sense of ending changes our past and our present by radically redefining our future.

In the warning of Jesus, the end of time reveals the meaning of time. Jesus warns us that we cannot know when the day of the Lord is coming. The great paradox of his warning is that the reign of God is both a present and a future reality. In a very real sense, in the sayings and stories of Jesus, the end of time is now. The Son of Man is here. The reign of God is in our midst.

Mahayana Buddhists insist on the complete presence right now of the ultimate state of enlightenment. From the point of view of enlightenment, the Buddhist can claim:

> Thus all things are the perfection of being, infinite perfection, unobscured perfection, unconditioned perfection. All things are enlightenment, for they must be recognized as without essential nature. . . . Thus those who seek for Nirvana are to be laughed at, for the man in the midst of birth-and-death is also seeking Nirvana.[95]

Buddhists acknowledge that it is, nonetheless, very difficult to arrive at the point of realizing the truth of enlightenment. Buddhists in their own way face a tension between an already present enlightenment (which is called "original enlightenment") and the stubborn experience of most of the human race who have not yet awakened.

The first of the pictures of the oxherd expresses this paradox in describing the beginning of the search for the ox. The animal, representing the true self, has never been lost, and yet the oxherd does not know the ox at all: "The beast has never gone astray, and what is the use of searching for him?" There is nothing to find, and yet there is a problem: "The reason why the oxherd is not on intimate terms with him is because the oxherd himself has violated his own inmost nature."[96]

In a similar vein, Dogen taught both that it is essential to practice meditation without ceasing and also that the first attempt to meditate, to do zazen, is already the attainment of enlightenment. The process is not accomplished only at the end of a long trial; the goal is already fully present at the very beginning efforts of the most rank novice. Christians watch for the coming of the Son of Man who has already come. Buddhists seek to awaken to the reality that they already are.

□   *A leper came to [Jesus]*
    [and kneeling down]
    begged him and said,

        "If you wish,
        you can make me clean."

    Moved with pity,
    he stretched out his hand,
    touched him,
    and said to him,

        "I do will it.
        Be made clean."

    The leprosy left him immediately,
    and he was made clean.

    Then, warning him sternly,
    he dismissed him at once.

    Then he said to him,

        "See that you tell no one
        anything." □

                    (Mark 1:40–44)

21 Silence

WHENEVER NINTH-CENTURY ZEN MASTER CHÜH-CHI (JAPANESE: GUTEI) WAS ASKED A QUESTION, such as, "What is the essence of Buddhism?", he would respond by raising one finger. When he was close to death, he told his fellow monks: "I attained Tenryu's [Chinese: T'ien-lung] Zen of One Finger. I used it all through my life, but could not exhaust it." Immediately after saying this, he died.[97] Shibayama comments: "[H]e could never put it in words even if he wished to do so. Or I might say he expressed it fully."[98] Silence was the only perfect expression.

When one of his students copied the master's one-finger response, however, Chüh-chi cut off the boy's finger with a knife. The boy ran away screaming. Chüh-chi called him. The boy turned to look, and Chüh-chi raised one finger. At that the boy was enlightened. The point of Zen is not to teach a model that can be imitated, but to awaken us to our own true self. The silence of enlightenment may appear simple, but it is very difficult to attain. It is not a matter of simply copying someone else.

A famous image that is very important to the Buddhist tradition presents a finger pointing to the moon. Buddhists warn that it would be a calamity to take the finger for the moon itself. Buddhism seeks to cut through words to direct experience, experience which is often best communicated in silence.

Jesus orders the leper he has healed to be silent about the miracle. The Gospel of Mark is a prolonged struggle with silence, a movement from one silence to another. Silence returns again and again on the journey from Jesus's baptism to his empty tomb, but always in a different form with a different meaning. The Gospel can be read as a journey into silence, and the main point of all its words is to bring us to the point of silence.

Jesus repeatedly orders people to be silent after a miracle. He does not want people to know who he is or what wonders have happened. Is it sheer perversity on Jesus's part? Or does Jesus's command to silence arise perhaps from the fear that the words that come will be the wrong words, the miracle story that will be told in excitement and amazement will be the wrong miracle story, that the wonder-worker that the crowds acclaim will not be the person Jesus truly is?

After a miracle, Jesus says, there should be silence. The role of a miracle is to initiate us into mystery, the mystery of the reign of God, and the proper response to mystery is silence. As one Zen master said when queried about enlightenment, "Anything I could possibly say would miss the point."

Silence changes its character during the course of the Gospel of Mark. It becomes both more frightening and more awesome. The failed silences after the miracles are first efforts to find silence—preparations for the real silences that will come later on: when Jesus prays in the Garden of Gethsemane, when he cries out from the cross, and when the women go away from the empty tomb in silence.

Jesus cries out in anguish to God both in the Garden and from the cross, and God is silent. In that silence of God there echo all the screams of those who have died unjustly, abandoned, alone, God-forsaken. When Jesus actually finds silence, it is terrifying. Yet out of that silence arises the only confession of Jesus in the Gospel of Mark which is not rebuked—from the Roman soldier who supervised his execution.

Shortly after the silence of God on the cross, the women at the tomb are given the opposite command—to go and tell the disciples of the resurrection. They go off in silence. The usual translation tells us that they were silent because they were afraid, but the Greek word *ephebounto* can perhaps be better translated as "they were in awe." Silence and awe are the proper response to mystery. At last, someone obeyed Jesus's earlier command: After a miracle, there should be silence. The oldest manuscripts of Mark's Gospel end at this point (16:8). For Mark, it is through the silence of the women that we hear the Gospel.

The silence of God, not unlike the silence of Buddhist enlightenment, echoes around us, echoes so loudly we cannot hear it. It plays with us, teases us, lures us forward to our death, a death that is our initiation into life.

□ *For whoever wishes*

to save his life

will lose it,

but

whoever loses his life

for my sake

will find it. □

(Matthew 16:25)

22 Know Thyself

C|ENTURIES AGO, IN THE T'ANG DYNASTY OF CHINA, A FAMOUS CONVERSATION OCCURRED about the basis of Zen Buddhist teaching. Nan-yüeh (677–744) asked the Zen master Hui-an (582–709):

> "What was in the mind of Bodhidharma when he came from India to China?"
> [Hui-an] answered, "Why not ask about your own mind?" . . .
> Then [Nan-yüeh] asked, "What is my own mind?" . . .
> The master gave [Nan-yüeh] a very subtle answer: "Look within, for something inscrutable is at work there."
> "What is that, Master?"
> The master gave him no further verbal answer. He simply opened his eyes and then closed them.[99]

Some time later, Nan-yüeh went to another Zen master, Hui Neng, in search of further wisdom. Hui Neng asked him: "Who is it that thus comes here?"

Nan-yüeh reflected upon this question for eight years. Finally he answered: "When one defines it as being a something, one has already missed the mark."[100]

The ancient Greeks also wrestled with the question of self-knowledge. In ancient times they erected a temple to the Greek god Apollo in Delphi, and people came from all over the Mediterranean world to consult the oracle at Delphi and seek wisdom. Various answers were given to the questions posed, but one word of advice was given to all: "Know thyself." This maxim is as brief as it can be, but it has served as one of the bases of Western thought.

It seems so simple. We all think that we do know ourselves. Yet the saying questions us critically: Do we really know ourselves? The maxim suggests that the only way to raise our consciousness is to begin by putting in question our normal consciousness of ourselves. It invites us to realize how we deceive ourselves by seeing what we want to see, hearing what we want to hear. To know ourselves requires a long roundabout path, a detour that begins with the questioning of our ordinary self-understanding.

The wisdom the maxim offers is the suggestion that we do what everyone takes for granted, but no one really does. If we presume that we do not know ourselves, then we can begin to discover who we are.

Buddhist teachers constantly warn their students that they do not know themselves. Zen masters advise their students: "Have an interview with who you were before you were even born." Zen teachers challenge us to seek the source of all experience prior to the divisions of the intellect, prior to the experience of subject and object, prior to the distorting lens of self-interest. As Loori puts it: "Self and other are not two. . . . The illusion of the self as a separate entity is what is not real."[101]

Jesus offers his followers a maxim of his own that is also a paradoxical challenge to our usual self-understanding. Jesus assumes that we all want to save our lives, that we all love our lives. But he warns us that this assumption turns quickly into its opposite. In trying to save our lives, in "loving" our lives, Jesus cautions, we are actually losing them. What we think is life is really death. What we think is success is bringing ourselves to ruin.

Jesus, like the Buddha, poses the question: What is our real life, our real salvation, our real identity?

PART III

Death and Resurrection and the Great Death

T HE CLIMAX OF THE SEARCH FOR THE SELF IN BUDDHISM IS A LETTING GO, A REALIZATION, AN awakening which the tradition of Rinzai Zen describes as "the Great Death" or "the Great Doubt." This is the moment when the searcher overcomes the separations and the dualities that have caused illusions. Students are told that they should

> inquire, with their heart and soul, what it is to transcend yes and no, you and I. They are to cast their whole being, from head to foot, into this inquiry and carry on with it. There will be no world, no self, but just one Great Doubt.[102]

This can be a frightening experience. According to Hakuin (1685–1768), "It was like sitting in an ice cave a million miles thick." Shibayama explains: "This is the moment when the I and the world are both altogether gone. This is exactly the moment when one's discriminating mind is emptied and cast away."[103]

This experience cannot be described in words: "Those who know it do not talk." The attempt to capture the experience in a theory or a concept is foolhardy:

> Even more foolish is one who clings to words and phrases and thus tries to achieve understanding. It is like trying to strike the moon with a stick, or scratching a shoe because there is an itchy spot on the foot. It has nothing to do with the Truth.[104]

Thus it was recounted that Shakyamuni Buddha sometimes taught with an air of resignation because he knew that his listeners could not understand what he was trying to communicate. It is impossible to capture the experience by parroting someone else's words. When a student mimicked someone else's poem, the Zen master asked him, "Where is your poem?" The student was dumbfounded.

The Great Death is not a new theory but a new way of experiencing ourselves and all things in the universe. As Merton commented, "Zen explains nothing. It just sees. Sees what? Not an Absolute Object but Absolute Seeing."[105]

The center of Christian experience is the death and resurrection of Jesus. This experience also surpasses the power of words. The images of death and rebirth are used for both Buddhist enlightenment and for Christian conversion, though in very different contexts. Jesus tells Nicodemus that he must be born again. Shibayama uses the image of rebirth to describe the heart of Zen: "One has to cast his ordinary self away and be reborn as a new Self in a different dimension. . . . This fundamental experience of awakening is essential in Zen."[106] The shattering experience of the Great Doubt or the Great Death is a breakthrough to liberation. The mind resides in emptiness but does not attach itself to emptiness.

For both religions the death of the self is an identification with a larger reality and an experience of liberation. Through conversion, Christians become one with Christ, so that Christ lives in us. In Buddhism the person becomes what Suzuki calls the "zero self," which is identified with the totality of infinity.[107]

There are, to be sure, fundamental differences between the two experiences. The central problem for the Christian is the burden of a real, sinful self that must die so that we can be born again in Christ. The central problem for the Buddhist is the erroneous belief in an inherently existing self that clings to desires and delusions. The Buddhist must let go of belief in the delusory self in order to awaken to the emptiness of the true self, the Buddha-nature. Through dying and rising with Christ, the Christian experiences a new way of being in the world which leads to a new way of knowing. The Buddhist experiences a new way of knowing the self which leads to a new way of being in the world. The Christian becomes one with Christ, while the Buddhist identifies not with the Buddha but with emptiness. In both cases, however, the death of the old self leads to a radical transformation of life.

☐ *Now there were some Greeks*
among those who had come up to worship
at the feast.

They came to Philip,
who was from Bethsaida in Galilee,
and asked him,

> *"Sir, we would like to see Jesus."*

Philip went and told Andrew;
then Andrew and Philip went and told Jesus.

Jesus answered them,

> *"The hour has come for the Son of Man*
> *to be glorified.*
>
> *Amen, amen, I say to you,*
> *unless a grain of wheat*
> *falls to the ground*
> *and dies,*
> *it remains just a grain of wheat;*
>
> *but if it dies,*
> *it produces much fruit."* ☐

(John 12:20–24)

23 The Self That Dies

A MONK ASKED CHAO-CHOU, "WHEN I BRING NOTHING AT ALL WITH ME, WHAT DO YOU SAY?"

Chao-Chou said, "Throw it away!"

"But," protested the monk, "I said I bring nothing at all; what do you say I should throw away?"

"Then carry it off," was the retort of Chao-Chou.[108]

At the center of Buddhism is the casting away of an illusory self that we never really possessed and the acceptance of the emptiness that we always have been. It is this experience that some Zen Buddhists call "the Great Death." Master Shido Bunan expressed it thus:

> Die while alive, and be completely dead,
> Then do whatever you will, all is good.[109]

Dogen explained the Great Death: "Death: just death all through—complete manifestation!" Shiba-

141

yama comments: "When you die, just die. When you just die thoroughly and completely you will have transcended life and death. Then, for the first time, free and creative Zen life and work will be developed."[110]

Chapter twelve of the Gospel of John presents Jesus wrestling with the meaning of his own imminent death. At this point in the Gospel of John, Jesus is famous for having raised Lazarus from the dead.

He is the wonder-worker who has power over death, and the Greeks who are visiting for the feast of Passover are curious and request to see him. Jesus's answer, however, is on a completely different level. It is as if he did not even hear the request. The everyday world of curious travelers seems unreal to Jesus. Perhaps the Greeks seeking to see him represent the side of us that wants to escape death.

Jesus's response warns that death is not something to be avoided. The death that Jesus is talking about is not just a future reality somewhere out there ahead of us. Jesus interprets death as bound up with the present moment. He speaks in the present tense of a present process: whoever loves his or her life loses it.

Jesus turns to the image of a grain of wheat to express this process, and imagines the grain facing a decision. As long as it remains a grain of wheat and holds onto its own life, it is just what it is. This life is so safe that it is a kind of living death. The grain of wheat by itself represents a vain and contradictory effort to hold onto its own life.

If the grain of wheat "dies" and is buried in the earth, a strange transformation occurs. The earth and water and sun begin to work on it, the grain is pulled out of itself, and dies. It disappears. Very soon there is no grain left, and in its place a process of new life has begun.

Jesus is suggesting that the meaning of our future physical death is related to the decision we make right now. We can cling selfishly to life, grasping at it for ourselves. In that case we have already lost our lives. Or we can accept the risk of going out of ourselves.

For Jesus, dying means serving; it means entering into relationships that will transform us. To let go of oneself is to accept death and transformation even now. For Jesus, death is the reality of the present moment, but it is a death which is already a participation in the resurrection. In an analogous way, the Great Death of Buddhism is a possibility of present transformation and a letting go of self—a challenge for life at the present moment.

□ *Abba, Father,*

    all things are possible

    to you.

Take this cup

    away from me,

      but not what I will

      but what you will. □

(Mark 14:36)

24 The Cup of Suffering

T HIS BRIEF PRAYER, ONE OF THE MOST MOVING EVER PRAYED, EXPRESSES THE CONFLICT WHICH runs throughout the story of the Passion of Jesus. On the one hand, Jesus prays to God as Father, as a loving, gracious God who never abandons us. On the other hand, Jesus acknowledges the cup, the cup of suffering which represents rejection and betrayal, torture and death.

The life of Jesus ends in the clash between these two images which seem so directly contradictory: If God is Father, why does Jesus have to drink the cup of suffering? If Jesus suffers, how can God be a loving and gracious Father? There is no theoretical answer given to the question. The resolution given is not in theory but in an act of consent: "not what I will but what you will."

The act of consent seems powerless; it seems only to acknowledge the inevitable outward course of events; it seems a surrender of freedom. Yet the para-

dox is that this act of consent transforms the meaning of
Jesus's suffering. It is an act not of despair but of
acceptance, not the destruction of freedom but its
establishment. It is precisely by saying "Yes" in the
midst of suffering that Jesus's death becomes a gift of
himself to us.

The Buddhist tradition does not face the question of suffering in quite the same way as the Christian
tradition. For Buddhists, the question of a gracious,
loving Father permitting suffering does not arise, for
ultimate reality in the Buddhist tradition is not encountered as a transcendent creator who can be addressed
in personal terms. For Buddhists, suffering is the inevitable result of our self-centered desires, of our attachments to this world and to ourselves. By cutting through
our attachments, we cut through the source of suffering. The transformation that this process brings about
enables us to enter into the suffering of others with
compassion.

Shakyamuni Buddha did not suffer as brutally
violent a death as Jesus (according to tradition, he died
after eating tainted meat that had been offered him). In
his own way, however, the Buddha freely entered into
suffering by postponing entrance into Nirvana and identifying with all beings in order to lead them to enlightenment. Siddhartha Gautama, after being enlightened and
becoming Shakyamuni Buddha, was tempted one last
time by Mara, the Lord of Desire, the tempter: "O holy
one, be pleased to enter Nirvana, thy desires are accomplished."[111] For the Buddha, a premature death appears
as an attractive invitation. The tempter speaks the last
temptation in a Buddhist voice, offering Shakyamuni
Buddha the experience of Nirvana that he had sought,
and Shakyamuni refuses.

Shakyamuni responded: "I will first establish in perfect wisdom worlds as numerous as the sand, and then I will enter Nirvana."[112] Christ accepts a premature death willingly to manifest God's forgiving love; the Buddha postpones death and entrance into Nirvana willingly so that he can enlighten countless other beings. While the outward expressions of the two religious leaders' concern are almost directly opposed, their lives are united by a desire to bring liberation to all.

The example of Christ has inspired Christians to follow what they understand God's will to be, even to the point of risking their lives for others. The example of Shakyamuni Buddha inspired the Mahayana Buddhist image of the bodhisattva, a being who enters into the suffering of other beings in order to release them from pain. In Mahayana Buddhism a "great bodhisattva" is a person who is able to achieve enlightenment and pass from the suffering of time into the peace of Nirvana. The great bodhisattva pauses on the threshold of Nirvana and resolves not to enter into peace until she or he can lead every other sentient being into Nirvana as well. The bodhisattva sacrifices her or his peace for the sake of others. D. T. Suzuki explains:

> A Bodhisattva would not seclude himself into the absolute tranquility of Nirvana, simply because he wishes to emancipate his fellow-creatures also from the bondage of ignorance and infatuation. . . . And this self-sacrifice, this unselfish devotion to the welfare of his fellow-beings constitutes the essence of Bodhisattvahood.[113]

In light of this figure, Buddhists sometimes interpret Jesus as a Bodhisattva who refused to escape suffering and chose to sacrifice himself for the sake of all beings.

□ *They gave him wine drugged with myrrh,*
  but he did not take it.

Then they crucified him
  and divided his garments by casting
  lots for them to see what each should take. . . .

And at three o'clock
  Jesus cried out in a loud voice,

    "Eloi, Eloi lema sabachthani?"

which is translated,

    "My God, my God, why have you forsaken
    me?" □

(Mark 15:23–24, 34)

25 Suffering and the Cross

T HE CROSS IS AS DISORIENTING AS A ZEN KOAN. IT IS PROBABLY FAMILIARITY WITH THE IMAGE THAT has dulled our sense of how strange it is to take the crucified Lord as the key to the meaning of God and ourselves. The negative side of the cross is shattering— the cross shatters our dreams, our desperate efforts to clutch at bits of meaning, and it confronts us with the ugly reality of human cruelty, physical torture, and execution.

The cross puts in question trust in government or religion, for it was the Roman legal system, renowned for its justice, and the Jewish religious authorities who collaborated in this execution. Even the best legal systems and religious structures can be destructive. The cross confronts us with the absurd, painful side of human existence.

The language used to express the moment seems contradictory. Jesus's cry is almost a Christian

koan: How can God abandon the Son of God? If in Jesus
we find the key to the nature of God, then God in some
way knows what it is like to feel abandoned. God suffers
with all who suffer unjustly. Even in the places where
God seems most absent, God is to be found.

A world which routinely tortures and exe-
cutes people for political purposes, a world which
allows thousands of people to die of hunger, malnutri-
tion, and dehydration is a world that is not yet saved.
But neither is it a world that is simply abandoned, for the
cross tells us that God has entered into even the most
painful, God-forsaken moments of human existence
and embraced them.

In risking ourselves, in giving of ourselves even
at the cost of our own lives, we may be struggling
against the way of this world, but we are moving with
the way of God. The cross reassures us that even if we,
like Jesus, end by being misunderstood, mocked, and
killed, a life lived in love will not have been in vain. The
cross is the sign both of human cruelty and also of the
depth of God's love. The overcoming of suffering, for the
Christian tradition, is found in God's entering into
human life, accepting human cruelty at its worst, and
embracing humankind and all creation in forgiving,
transforming love.

The Buddhist tradition is also acutely aware of
the suffering of human life. Indeed, the first of the Four
Noble Truths of Shakyamuni Buddha proclaims that life
is suffering (*dukkha*), that is, impermanent, culminating
in death and decay. The attempt to deny the reality of
suffering is itself a delusion that blocks the path to
wisdom, and a harsh encounter with suffering can
sometimes be the stimulus needed to seek enlightenment. It was only when Siddhartha left the sheltered

world of his father's palace and saw a sick man, an old man, a dead man, and a mendicant that he became dissatisfied with his life of comfort and security and began to seek wisdom.

Shakyamuni learned that the cause of suffering is our craving for things, our clinging to desires, our being addicted to some aspect of life's pleasures. This is the Second Noble Truth. Freedom from such addictions brings freedom from suffering. When we no longer cling to our desires, we are free to experience life as it is. This is the Third Noble Truth. The last of the Four Noble Truths indicates that the path to such freedom is a middle way between extremes, a path based upon a proper view of all things and proper conduct towards all.

The Christian tradition confronts the paradox of a world that is already redeemed by God but that is still dominated by sin and needless suffering two thousand years after the death of Christ. The harsh reality of the cross and the continuing violence in the present are abrupt reminders that the transformation of the world has not yet been completed. While the Christian has already experienced God's love overcoming suffering, nonetheless the tragedies of history demonstrate graphically that grace has not yet triumphed completely.

There is also a paradoxical dialectic of enlightenment already present and not yet attained in Buddhist experience. In the Buddhist tradition the overcoming of suffering comes with enlightenment. As we have seen, when Shakyamuni was enlightened, he realized that all beings are always already enlightened. Nonetheless, human aggression continues the seemingly endless horrors of history. When we awaken, we realize who we have always been, and yet our world is still trapped by the power of the three poisons of ignorance, anger, and greed.

Two images have been etched in the memories of their respective traditions: Jesus Christ hanging on the cross and Shakyamuni Buddha seated in lotus position, extending a blessing of peace to the world. A violent, senseless death, and a peaceful invitation to enlightenment. A classic image of love and a classic image of compassion: a Savior lays down his life, and a Teacher enlightens all sentient beings to their true nature. While the two figures respond to the crisis of human suffering in very different ways, both images represent a process of reconciliation, of coming into harmony with ultimate reality, with our deepest nature and with the universe around us.

☐ On the first day of the week, Mary of Magdala
came to the tomb early in the morning,
while it was still dark,
and saw the stone removed from the tomb.
So she ran and went to Simon Peter
and to the other disciple whom Jesus loved,
and told them,

> "They have taken the Lord from the tomb,
> and we don't know where they put him."

So Peter and the other disciple went out and
came to the tomb. They both ran, but the
other disciple ran faster than Peter
and arrived at the tomb first; he bent down
and saw the burial cloths there,
but did not go in.

When Simon Peter arrived after him,
he went into the tomb and saw the burial cloths
there, and the cloth that had covered his head,
not with the burial cloths
but rolled up in a separate place.

Then the other disciple also went in,
the one who had arrived at the tomb first,
and he saw and believed.

For they did not yet understand the scripture
that he had to rise from the dead. ☐

(John 20:1–9)

26 Signs of Resurrection

T HE TRADITION OF ZEN BUDDHISM HAS LONG USED KOANS TO CHALLENGE THE UNDERSTAND-ing of students. Koans do not answer our problems for us, but challenge us to reflect, to see in a new way, to experience in a different fashion. Koans both express and provoke the experience of the Great Death. The signs of Jesus in the Gospel of John are in some respects not unlike the koans of the Buddhists.

The Gospel of John presents itself as a book of signs. From the first miracle at Cana through the feeding of the multitude, the healing of the blind man, the resurrection of Lazarus, and the Last Supper, there occurs one sign after the other. The Gospel of John always calls the miracles of Jesus "signs."

Strange things happen in the stories of these signs. They are not just external signs pointing some-where else. All of them are signs of transformation, signs that break into people's lives, turn their lives around, and leave them different persons than before.

A sign initiates a person into a deeper level of reality. But signs are ambiguous. Like Zen koans, they do not yield their meaning easily and directly. They demand that we participate in the creation of meaning, and so they confront us with a choice. They challenge our self-understanding, tease our minds, and prod us to reflection and wonder. They also provoke very different reactions: because of the signs Jesus works, some people believe and find life; others want to put him to death.

Interpreting a sign is like answering the riddle of the sphinx. If you understand, you live. If you do not, you die.

The last and greatest of the signs of Jesus in the Gospel of John is the sign of the resurrection. John approaches the story slowly, giving us time to ponder the sign. There is no account of the angel coming down and moving away the stone. There is no flash of lightning. Instead we find signs that are ambiguous, that raise questions, that need to be interpreted.

Mary Magdelene arrives at the tomb when it is still dark. In darkness we are disoriented and easily lost. In darkness we have trouble seeing the realities around us. The sign is first revealed in darkness. In John, the Gospel which says so much about the struggle against darkness, the time of the resurrection is a time shrouded in darkness.

Mary does not see an angel, only a stone rolled away and an empty tomb. She can penetrate the meaning of the sign only through interpreting the emptiness of the tomb and the absence of the body in the early morning darkness. First Jesus died. Now even his body is gone. The first sign that Mary encounters is emptiness and absence.

But Mary Magdelene does not know how to interpret the sign. She races to tell the others. It is as if the interpretation of this sign demands a community. One individual alone cannot decipher it. Mary tells Peter and the beloved disciple, "The Lord has been taken from the tomb! We don't know where they have put him!" The way Mary announces the resurrection is as a riddle, a puzzle that she cannot solve.

For their part, Peter and the beloved disciple race to the tomb and look in and peer into the emptiness, the absence. It is in the silence, the emptiness, the absence that the beloved disciple believes; he believes without as yet understanding.

"He saw and believed." Four words that point to what cannot be said. The very next line tells us that he did not understand, but his life was forever changed. The meaning of his life was from then on related to the meaning of this emptiness, this absence; his vocation was to be a witness to the resurrection—an apostle.

In the Gospel of John, the beloved disciple believes without seeing the risen Lord and without understanding. The special concern of the Fourth Gospel is for "those who have not seen," that means, for us. In a special way, this Gospel is a Gospel for the people who have never seen an angel sitting on a tomb, for people who live in a world of ambiguity in a time of darkness, a world where God is often experienced as absent.

The first signs given to Mary, to Peter, and to the beloved disciple are, in a sense, the signs given to us. For Christians of later generations, there is no immediate vision, no angel's voice, no direct appearance of

Jesus himself: only the realities of our ordinary world, strangely transformed because the Lord has been here. This tomb and these wrappings speak of the Lord so loudly that the beloved disciple believes. Because of the presence in absence of the risen Lord, they are transformed into signs of the resurrection, transfiguring our world.

There is no one historical moment which has a comparable significance for Buddhists. The key to the nature of reality for Buddhists is not the death and resurrection of a Savior but rather the awakening of Shakyamuni Buddha—an awakening which is a real possibility for every human person. The enlightenment of the Buddha did not change the outward appearance of the things of the universe. And yet, as we have seen, when the Buddha attained enlightenment all the things of the universe attained enlightenment with him and thus have the power to enlighten his followers. The ordinary realities of everyday life are ambiguous for the Buddhist: they can be taken as independently existing objects for our desire and control, or they can be experienced as manifestations of emptiness, of the Buddha-nature which all things are. A Japanese Buddhist, Daio (1235–1308), expressed his experience of enlightenment:

> No longer aware of mind and object,
> I see earth, mountains, rivers at last.
> The Dharmakaya's* everywhere.
> Worldlings, facing it, can't make it out.[114]

---

* The cosmic body of the Buddha or Buddha-nature.

☐ *On the evening of that first day of the week,*
when the doors were locked, where the disciples were,
for fear of the Jews, Jesus came
and stood in their midst and said to them,

> *"Peace be with you."*

When he had said this,
he showed them his hands and his side.
The disciples rejoiced when they saw the Lord.
[Jesus] said to them again,

> *"Peace be with you.*
> *As the Father has sent me, so I send you."*

And when he had said this,
he breathed on them and said to them,

> *"Receive the holy Spirit.*
> *Whose sins you forgive are forgiven them, and*
> *whose sins you retain are retained."*

Thomas, called Didymus, one of the Twelve,
was not with them when Jesus came.
So the other disciples said to him,

> *"We have seen the Lord."*

But he said to them,
> *"Unless I see the mark of the nails in his hands*
> *and put my finger into the nailmarks*
> *and put my hand into his side,*
> *I will not believe."* ☐

(John 20:19–25)

27 The Experience of Healing

S HAKYAMUNI BUDDHA HAD A COUSIN NAMED
DEVADATTA WHO BECAME HIS MOST BITTER
enemy and betrayer. Devadatta was jealous of the reverence people felt for his cousin and desired to usurp his
place. He spread slander about Shakyamuni with the
intention of trapping him. He tried to kill Shakyamuni
Buddha by rolling a boulder down a road where he was
traveling. Another time Devadatta made an elephant
drunk, hoping that it would run amok and kill the
Buddha. On still other occasions, he gave poison to the
Buddha and shot at him with his bow. Devadatta was a
most determined and ferocious enemy.

The Lotus Sutra tells us that Shakyamuni
predicted: "Devadatta, after his departure and innumerable kalpas [immense periods of time] have passed, will
become a buddha. . . . He shall widely preach the Wonderful Law for all the living."[115] In this astonishing
prediction Shakyamuni affirmed that even the most

wicked and treacherous person possesses the Buddha-nature and can in time become free of delusion and become a great teacher and Buddha. No matter how bitter the offenses Devadatta had committed, he could attain enlightenment and benefit countless beings.

Shakyamuni also gave his followers an example of forgiving compassion. Not only did Shakyamuni show no resentment for Devadatta, he even praised him and attributed his own enlightenment "to the good friendship of Devadatta." Shakyamuni explained that it was Devadatta who enabled him to become perfect "in kindness, compassion, joy, and indifference . . . the attainment of Perfect Enlightenment, and the wide-spread saving of the living."[116] The injuries that Devadatta had sought to inflict upon the Buddha were in fact helpful to him. Far from seeking revenge and judgment, Shakyamuni showed only compassion and gratitude to his devious cousin. Enlightenment and forgiveness are inseparable.

In the resurrection accounts of the Gospel of John, we find two questions closely intertwined: Is Jesus really risen? Can I really forgive and be forgiven and be at peace? Those two questions seem at first to be very different, but both pose a challenge to our belief. The claim of the resurrection may appear to be more difficult to believe. It seems to be a matter of sheer speculation beyond any possibility of proof. The second claim—that sins can be forgiven—may be actually more difficult to answer in practice. The Gospel story suggests that the two questions are very closely linked.

The suffering of the cross had posed a tremendous challenge to the faith of the disciples. Their hopes seemed to have been misplaced. The violent death of Jesus poses a basic question about the meaning of reality: Is life an absurd and terrifying nightmare or is the ultimate meaning of reality found in reconciliation? In a world of crucifixions, can one believe in the possibility of healing and being healed?

Thomas approaches the question of the resurrection in terms of experience. Unless he experiences the Risen Lord, he will not believe. The doubting Thomas knows that the cross is real. He knows all too well the fearful power of suffering and the danger of deception. He fears that the hope of the resurrection is misplaced and that life ends in unresolved conflict.

When Jesus appears to the disciples, his very first word is "Peace." The first message of the Risen Lord is one of forgiveness and acceptance. He does not ask his friends why they ran away. He does not berate them for abandoning him, nor does he scold Peter for denying that he knew him. He rather breathes on them and challenges them to forgive others. As he has forgiven them, so they are to forgive others. Forgiving people, healing hurts is a human responsibility. Resurrection and forgiveness are inseparable.

For Buddhists, the experience of enlightenment is a reconciliation with all reality. It entails letting go of past hurts and the desire to take revenge. It also means accepting forgiveness for ourselves. In enlightenment, Dogen comments, the Buddhas and ancestors "have compassion for me, deliver me from karmic shackles [burdens formed by past sins], and eliminate any hindrances to my learning of the Way."[117] To realize emptiness is to be freed from the chains of past injuries and cast off the traces of past evil deeds.

The friendship of the Buddha with Devadatta and the friendship of Jesus with his weak-willed disciples pose a radical challenge to their followers. To follow the way of the Buddha or the way of Christ is to accept the reality of forgiveness.

While the Christian tradition acknowledges the real threat of human freedom in traditional images of hell, the best of the tradition has refused to declare that any persons actually are separated from God's love forever. Even the fate of Judas Iscariot cannot be known with certitude. As the Lotus Sutra describes the hope of the Buddha for reconciliation with his betrayer, so an old Christian ballad tells the legend of Judas Iscariot.

After the death of Judas, his soul carried his body throughout the universe seeking a place to rest. Neither heaven nor earth nor even hell would accept it. Finally the soul of Judas came upon a lighted hall where a banquet was taking place. Jesus waited inside, hoping that his betrayer would at last make his peace with him. Jesus opened the door to welcome his betrayer and invited him to join the celebration:

> The Holy Supper is spread within,
> And the many candles shine,
> And I have waited long for thee
> Before I poured the wine![118]

Conclusion:
Life Transformed

T|HE GOAL OF BOTH BUDDHISM AND CHRISTIAN-
ITY IS LIFE TRANSFORMED. THE EXPERIENCE OF
death and rebirth—whether through the Buddhist's enlightenment or the Christian's union with Jesus
Christ—leaves a person profoundly changed. The enlightened life, for a follower of the Buddha, is marked,
above all, by wisdom and compassion. The Christian
life is marked, in St. Paul's classic description, by faith,
hope, and love.

While Buddhism and Christianity understand
the human predicament and the path to freedom in
strikingly different ways, both traditions agree that our
ordinary life is deluded and dominated by a false self
that must die. For the Buddhist, life before enlightenment is dominated by the three poisons of ignorance,
anger, and greed. All three find their source of strength
in the delusion that one exists as a separate, independent self over against the rest of the universe. As long as

one clings to this delusion, enslaving desires and need-less sufferings are inevitable results. The destructive conflicts, anxieties, and drives that plague human rela-tionships all arise from the delusion of an independent self.

Where Buddhists describe the fundamental problem of human existence as ignorance of our true nature, Christians speak of sin as rejection of God's call. Different as the two descriptions are, they nonetheless agree in challenging our ordinary patterns of acting and thinking. The Buddhist understanding of life before enlightenment—a self divided against itself, driven to and fro by desires—can be compared with Augustine's description of human life dominated by *cupiditas*—the self-seeking, self-destructive love of self that de-vours human life apart from grace. The Buddhist experi-ence of life poisoned by ignorance, greed, and anger is not unlike Augustine's experience of the battle be-tween disorderly, irrational appetites that delude and destroy us.

While the paths to transformation are rather different for Buddhists and Christians, there are none-theless many themes common to both traditions. The roles played by the founders of the two traditions contrast sharply. The Christian finds life transformed through an encounter with the historical bearer of salvation, Jesus Christ. In and through the life, death, and resurrection of Jesus Christ, the Christian experi-ences the love of God transforming human existence. This love, which extends throughout all human experi-ence and the entire cosmos, is specially revealed in Jesus Christ and in the ongoing life of the Christian Church.

Where Christians find in Jesus Christ the decisive manifestation of the power of God's love, Buddhists awaken to the Buddha-nature that they have always had. The historical person, Shakyamuni Buddha, is a teacher and guide, but he is not a redeemer from sin, and he is not the revelation of a creating God.

Both the names of Christ and Buddha, however, do come to be applied on a cosmic scale, far beyond their original historical bearers. Since Jesus Christ is the incarnation of the divine Word active throughout the universe in creation, "Christ" comes to name the power of God at work throughout the cosmos, holding all things together (Colossians 1:15–17). Thus Christ comes to name the reality of God's love that we have always experienced, whether we have been explicitly conscious of it or not. The name "Buddha" comes to be applied to the nature of reality, which is emptiness, or the Buddha-nature. Thus, all human persons are called to realize the Buddhahood that they already share.

For the Christian tradition, transformation is experienced as a gift of grace from God who takes the initiative to call together a community of faith and love. Buddhists describe the experience of transformation in various ways, some of which resemble the Christian experience of grace. As we have seen, Shin Buddhists question the path of self-reliance and place their trust in the compassionate vow of Amida Buddha. Many Zen and Shin Buddhists see the opposition between self-power and other-power as a false dichotomy which is overcome in Other-Power. The Other-Power of Amida Buddha is experienced as a gracious gift which overcomes our sinfulness and offers us peace. In enlightenment the very idea of a separation between self-power and Other-Power is meaningless. As the Japanese Buddhist Saichi (1851–1933) expressed it:

There is no self-power
No other power
All is Other Power.[119]

The Christian experience of grace also involves an overcoming of the dichotomy between God and ourselves, between God's action and our action. As Paul wrote: "yet I live, no longer I, but Christ lives in me" (Galatians 2:20). Even though there are clear similarities between the two traditions, the experiences are not exactly the same. Shin Buddhists, despite their awe before the gift of the universe and their stress on our inability to save ourselves and the necessity of relying upon Other-Power, do not believe in a creating and redeeming God in the Christian sense. Amida Buddha is a name for emptiness or the Buddha-nature, which is ultimately not other than ourselves. While the role of Other-Power for Shin Buddhists is somewhat analogous to the Christian experience of God's grace, Other-Power cannot be simply identified with the reality that Christians name God.

The heart of Buddhist wisdom is the "casting off of body and mind"—the forgetting of the self and the realization that there is no separation between ourselves and the universe. Once the delusion of the inherently existing self is cast aside, the three poisons are overcome: ignorance becomes realization, anger becomes wisdom, and greed becomes compassion. Even though nothing outwardly has changed, everything has changed because we experience the universe differently. Buddhists stress that this transformation must be experienced to be understood. The new perspective on life is not simply a new intellectual theory, though it does have profound implications for our understanding of reality.

For Buddhists, words seem futile to express what happens in enlightenment. When Te-shan (782–865) was enlightened, he gathered together all his commentaries on the Diamond Sutra and burned them. When Pai-chang was asked to preach on the meaning of Buddhism to a group of monks, he told them first to go work on their farm and then he would preach. When they returned from their work, he said not a word but silently extended his arms towards the monks. The Chinese Zen Buddhist, Chang-ching (854–932), warned anyone who might ask him about enlightenment:

> Rolling the bamboo blind, I
> Look out at the world—what change!
> Should someone ask what I've discovered,
> I'll smash this whisk against his mouth.[120]

A long tradition of Christian theology insists that words are fundamentally inadequate to express the experience of God transforming human life. The mystical theologian Pseudo-Dionysius warned: "Nor can any words come up to the inexpressible Good, the One, this Source of all unity, this supra-existent Being. Mind beyond mind, word beyond speech, it is gathered up by no discourse, by no intuition, by no name."[121] According to Pseudo-Dionysius, the height of worship is silence: "With a wise silence we do honor to the inexpressible."[122]

Pseudo-Dionysius describes the experience of God in language that in many ways resembles Buddhist accounts. The encounter with God is beyond the dualities we normally take for granted; it is a paradoxical knowing beyond all knowing: "Here, being neither oneself nor someone else, one is supremely united by a completely unknowing inactivity of all knowledge, and knows beyond the mind by knowing nothing."[123] For Pseudo-Dionysius, all divisions are overcome in a union beyond description.

For Christians, the heart of the experience of God and the ultimate criterion for all decisions is love. Paul warns against relying on special gifts or ecstatic experiences if they do not lead to love. Indeed, according to Paul, nothing else really matters if we do not have love (1 Corinthians 13:1-13). For Buddhists, awakening to the emptiness of ourselves and of all things in the universe overcomes the self-seeking desires that cause suffering. Having let go of the false dichotomies that separate us from other beings, we are filled with compassion for every other being. Compassion is not a task at which the truly enlightened Buddhist must work. It arises as naturally as the hair that grows on our heads.

Paul rejoices that the experience of God's grace brings a new freedom: "For freedom Christ set us free" (Galatians 5:1). This freedom is not an end in itself, however. Its purpose is service: "But do not use this freedom as an opportunity for the flesh; rather, serve one another through love. For the whole law is fulfilled in one statement, namely, 'You shall love your neighbor as yourself'" (Galatians 5:13-14). The Buddhist also finds a new freedom in enlightenment. Precisely because there is no inherent self to feel anxious over, the Buddhist experiences a tremendous sense of liberation and confidence. The enlightened Zen monk is described as roaming about like a golden-haired lion. Suzuki describes life after enlightenment as "more satisfying, more peaceful, and fuller of joy than anything you ever had. The tone of your life is altered. There is something rejuvenated in it."[124]

For Buddhists, this is the moment of returning to one's own home. Having found one's place in the jewel-net of Indra, there is no more cause for worry or alarm. There is no place in the universe in which we can get lost:

> Does one really have to fret
> About enlightenment?
> No matter what road I travel,
> I'm going home.[125]

Zen teachers explain this experience: "You have now found yourself; from the very beginning nothing has been kept away from you. It was yourself that closed the eye to the fact."[126]

The experience of liberation in both the Buddhist and Christian traditions involves a process of recognizing that we have been separated from our true home—the place of genuine meaning and freedom. In both traditions we have become lost through ignorance and sin. And yet, for both traditions, the recognition that we are lost also involves the insight that our true home has been within us all the time. The Christian has always lived in the love of God, no matter how blind the Christian may have been to that love. Indeed, God is closer to us than we are to ourselves. The Christian has always been the image of God, no matter how disguised and disfigured the image may have become. The Buddhist has lacked nothing from the very beginning and has always possessed the fullness of the Buddha-nature and original enlightenment, no matter how poisoned life may have become through ignorance, anger, and greed. For both traditions, the awakening to our true identity involves a painful process of dying but leads to a freedom and a delight in relation to the world, to others, and to ourselves.

As Paul warned that Christian freedom is not for selfish pleasure, so for Buddhists enlightenment cannot be an end in itself. Wisdom is inseparable from compassion, and so Buddhist teachers warn their students not to get "stuck" in enlightenment. Any student who wishes to cling to the experience of enlightenment for its own sake has not truly awakened. The ultimate goal of enlightenment is to share liberation with all other beings.

The actions and the parables of Jesus present a gracious but unpredictable God who welcomes sinners and outcasts but confronts the self-righteous. The playfulness of Jesus in overturning people's expectations finds a counterpart in the playfulness of the Zen masters who refuse the predictable and the routine. The playful side of Jesus's teaching challenges Christians to let go of the desire to control the process of salvation. God's welcome is consistently wider than people expect.

Paul interpreted the transformation of the Christian as a sharing in the death of Christ—a loss of self which leads to the freedom of the children of God. Paul knew very well that merely striving to follow the law can never save us. It is only through God's grace that the power of faith, working through love, can transform us.

Buddhists also know that the desire-ridden self can never save itself—in some way the self must die. In both the Buddhist and Christian traditions, discovering who we are requires an experience of letting go. In the search for our true identity, both traditions presuppose the precepts of morality but refuse to identify true human fulfillment with merely following rules externally imposed. Both traditions challenge us to discipline our desires and also to let go of our striving for dominance and control over others and ourselves.

Like Paul, the Gospel of John places the experience of love at the heart of the process of transformation. In the discourse at the Last Supper in the Fourth Gospel, Jesus sums up his entire message: "love one another as I love you" (John 15:12).

Augustine drew from both Paul and John in interpreting his own experience of sin and grace. If the Buddhist description of ignorance could be compared to Augustine's account of sinful self-love, the Buddhist experience of enlightenment can be compared to Augustine's description of the life of *caritas*—the love of God that restores us to ourselves, healing and transforming us. By ourselves, Augustine learned, we are powerless to escape from our warped and twisted self-love. It is only in surrendering the striving of our selfish desires that we find peace in God. What results for the Christian is a freedom in relating to others and to all creation—a freedom that cannot be fully captured in a series of rules. With the decentering of the self and its union with God, Augustine discovered only one command to be essential: "Love, and do what you will."

In the end, for the Christian, the most important experience is love. For the Buddhist, what is most important is compassion for all beings. The hallmark of both Christian love and Buddhist compassion is joy.

Two images from the Christian and Buddhist traditions capture the joyous celebration that results from life transformed. Jesus dines with tax-collectors and prostitutes in a banquet that celebrates the inbreaking of the reign of God into this world. The Buddhist oxherd who has been enlightened returns to the city to celebrate with the butchers and wine-drinkers, and all enjoy enlightenment together.

Both celebrations rejoice in overcoming the barriers that have divided us from one another and from our true home. Seng-t'san (d. 606) expressed the Buddhist experience:

> One in All,
> All in One—
> If only this is realized,
> No more worry about your not being perfect!
>
> Where Mind and each believing mind are not divided,
> And undivided are each believing mind and Mind,
> This is where words fail;
> For it is not of the past, present, and future.[127]

Paul describes the goal of the Christian experience:

> For [Christ] must reign until he has put all his enemies under his feet . . . When everything is subjected to him, then the Son himself will [also] be subjected to the one who subjected everything to him, so that God may be all in all (1 Corinthians 15:25, 28).

Notes

1. Wilfred Cantwell Smith, *Towards a World Theology: Faith and the Comparative History of Religions* (Philadelphia: Westminster Press, 1981), 7–9. Josaphat was also honored as St. Joasaph. See Aloysius Pieris, *Love Meets Wisdom: A Christian Experience of Buddhism* (Maryknoll, NY: Orbis Books, 1988), 25–26.
2. The name appears in the Bible as Jehoshaphat ("Yahweh is judge") in 1 Kings 15:24 and elsewhere. The Greek form is Josaphat in Matthew 1:8.
3. Smith, 20.
4. Arnold Toynbee, *Christianity among the Religions of the World* (New York: Charles Scribner's Sons, 1957), 102.
5. Vatican II, *Nostra Aetate (Declaration on the Relation of the Church to Non-Christian Religions),* No. 2; in *Vatican Council II: The Conciliar and Post Conciliar Documents,* ed. Austin Flannery (Collegeville, MN: Liturgical Press, 1984), 739.
6. *Bulletin of the North American Board for East-West Dialogue* 31 (1988): 1.
7. I will borrow one story from the early Theravada tradition, and will occasionally turn also to other figures in the Mahayana Buddhist tradition such as Kukai, the founder of Shingon Buddhism in Japan, and Fa-tsang, a leader of the Hua-yen school of Buddhism in China. Images of the Hua-yen school of Buddhism (Japanese: Kegon) are especially important for understanding Zen Buddhism. According to D. T. Suzuki, "the philosophy of Zen is Kegon and the teaching of Kegon bears its fruit in the life of Zen." (Introduction to Beatrice Lane Suzuki, *Mahayana Bud-*

176   *Life Transformed*

dhism (London, 1948), iv; quoted by Heinrich Dumoulin, *Zen Buddhism: A History,* Vol. 1: *India and China,* trans. James W. Heisig and Paul Knitter (New York: Macmillan Publishing Company, 1988), 46. In this book, I will give names in their original pronunciation except where the usual convention in English is otherwise. Thus, Ch'an Buddhism will be referred to under its Japanese pronunciation, "Zen."

8. Michael Pye, *Skilful Means: A Concept in Mahayana Buddhism* (London: Duckworth, 1978), 4.

9. Paul Ricoeur, "Beyond Autonomy and Heteronomy," Lecture at the University of Chicago (1987), 1.

10. Augustine, *Confessions* 1:2, trans. R. S. Pine-Coffin (Harmondsworth, England: Penguin Books, 1961), 22.

11. See Francis H. Cook, *Hua-yen Buddhism: The Jewel Net of Indra* (University Park, PA: Pennsylvania State University Press, 1977), 2; and Garma C. C. Chang, *The Buddhist Teaching of Totality: The Philosophy of Hwa Yen Buddhism* (University Park, PA: Pennsylvania State University Press, 1986), 165–66.

12. Fa-Tsang, *On the Golden Lion,* quoted by Chang, 24.

13. Kukai, *Kobo daishi zenshu,* 1:516; quoted by Yoshito S. Hakeda, *Kukai: Major Works, Translated, with an Account of His Life and a Study of His Thought* (New York: Columbia University Press, 1972), 92–93.

14. Daisetz Teitaro Suzuki, *An Introduction to Zen Buddhism* (New York: Grove Press, Inc., 1964), 39.

15. Manshi Kiyozawa, "The Great Path of Absolute Other-Power," in *The Buddha-Eye: An Anthology of the Kyoto School,* ed. Frederick Franck (New York: Crossroad, 1982), 233.

16. Ibid., 233–34.

17. Dogen, *Shobogenzo,* "Genjo Koan," quoted by Robert Aitken, "The Way of Dogen Zenji," Foreword to Hee-Jin Kim, *Dogen Kigen: Mystical Realist* (rev. ed.; Tucson, AZ: University of Arizona Press, 1987), xii.

18. Dogen, *Shobogenzo,* "Genjo-koan," trans. by Kim, *Dogen Kigen,* 100.

19. "Dogen's Bendowa," trans. Norman Waddell and Masao Abe, *The Eastern Buddhist* 4 (1971): 135, 136.

20. Daisetz Teitaro Suzuki, *Essays in Zen Buddhism: First Series* (New York: Grove Press, 1949; 1985), 230.

21. Masao Abe, "Man and Nature in Christianity and Buddhism," *The Buddha Eye,* 151.

22. Kiyozawa, "The Great Path of Absolute Other-Power," *The Buddha Eye,* 234.

23. Ibid.

24. Sosan, "On Believing in Mind," 25, in Daisetz Teitaro Suzuki, *Manual of Zen Buddhism* (New York: Grove Press, Inc., 1960), 81.

25. Douglas A. Fox, *The Heart of Buddhist Wisdom: A Translation of the Heart Sutra With Historical Introduction and Commentary,* Studies in Asian Thought and Religion, Vol. 3 (Lewiston, NY: Edwin Mellen Press, 1985), 87.

26. Ibid., 78.

27. From *Astasahasrika Prajnaparamita,* 7: 170–71; in *The Buddhist Tradition in India, China and Japan,* ed. Wm. Theodore de Bary (New York: Vintage Books, 1972), 103–04.

28. Rahulabhadra, "Hymn to Perfect Wisdom," 11, in *Buddhist Scriptures,* ed. and trans. Edward Conze (Harmondsworth, England: Penguin, 1959), 169.

29. Ibid.

30. Ibid., 170.

31. Abe, "Man and Nature in Christianity and Buddhism," *The Buddha Eye,* 151.

32. Suzuki, *Manual of Zen Buddhism,* 50.

33. Dogen, *A Primer of Soto Zen: A Translation of Dogen's Shobogenzo Zuimonki,* trans. Reiho Masunaga, An East-West Center Book (Honolulu: University of Hawaii Press, 1985), 50–51.

34. Daisetz Teitaro Suzuki, "What Is the 'I'?" *The Buddha Eye,* 45.

35. Suzuki, *Essays in Zen Buddhism,* 319.

36. Dogen, *Moon in a Dewdrop: Writings of Zen Master Dogen,* ed. Kazuaki Tanashi, trans. Robert Aitken et al. (San Francisco: North Point Press, 1985), 44–45.

37. Ibid., 46–47.

38. John Daido Loori, "The Miracle of Aliveness: A Dharma Discourse on Body Practice," *Mountain Record* 7, no. 1 (1988): 5–6.

39. Dogen, *Moon in a Dewdrop,* 45.

40. Dumoulin, 1:91.

41. Quoted by Yoshinori Takeuchi, *The Heart of Buddhism: In Search of the Timeless Spirit of Primitive Buddhism,* ed. and trans. James W. Heisig (New York: Crossroad, 1983), 76.

42. Suzuki, *Essays in Zen Buddhism,* 25.

43. Zenkei Shibayama, *Zen Comments on the Mumonkan,* trans. Sumiko Kudo (San Francisco: Harper & Row, 1984), 21.

44. Ibid., 22.

45. Suzuki, *Manual of Zen Buddhism,* 127–28.

46. Ibid., 117.

47. Ibid., 27.

48. Dogen, *Fukanzazengi: The Universal Promotion of the Principles of Zazen,* quoted by John Daido Loori, "Zazen: The Still Point," *Mountain Record* 6, no. 3 (1987): 7.

49. *Zen Poems of China and Japan: The Crane's Bill,* trans. Lucien Stryk et al. (Garden City, NY: Anchor Books, 1973), 49.

50. Alfred Bloom, *Shinran's Gospel of Pure Grace,* Monographs of the Association for Asian Studies, No. 20 (Tucson, AZ: University of Arizona Press, 1965), 1-4.

51. Gutoku Shaku Shinran, *The Kyogyoshinsho: The Collection of Passages Expounding the True Teaching, Living, Faith, and Realizing of the Pure Land,* ed. Eastern Buddhist Society, trans. Daisetz Teitaro Suzuki (Kyoto: Shinshu Otaniha, 1973), 229.

52. The Nishi Hongwanji Commission on the Promotion of Religious Education, *Shinran in the Contemporary World* (2nd ed.; Kyoto: Hongwanji International Center, 1979), 81.

53. Shinran, *Kyogyoshinsho,* 230.

54. Suzuki, *Essays in Zen Buddhism,* 9.

55. Hajime Tanabe, *Philosophy as Metanoetics,* trans. Yoshinori Takeuchi et al. (Berkeley: University of California Press, 1986).

56. Ibid., 9.

57. Athanasius, *On the Incarnation,* 54, trans. Penelope Lawson (New York: Macmillan Publishing Company, 1946), 86.

58. Augustine, *The Spirit and the Letter,* 60; in *Augustine: Later Works,* trans. John Burnaby (Philadelphia: Westminster Press, 1955), 245.

59. *Confessions,* 13:31.

60. Nicholas of Cusa, *On God as Not-other: A Translation and an Appraisal of De Li Non Aliud,* trans. Jasper Hopkins (Minneapolis: University of Minnesota Press, 1979).

61. Suzuki, *Essays in Zen Buddhism,* 370.

62. Shibayama, 15.

63. Joachim Jeremias, *The Parables of Jesus,* trans. S. H. Hooke (rev. ed.; New York: Charles Scribner's Sons, 1963), 132-33.

64. Ibid., 133.

65. Suzuki, *Essays in Zen Buddhism,* 376.

66. *The Buddha-karita of Asvaghosha,* trans. E. B. Cowell, in *Buddhist Mahayana Texts,* ed. E. B. Cowell et al., The Sacred Books of the East, vol. 49, ed. F. Max Müller (Oxford: Clarendon Press, 1894; reprint, New York: Dover Publications, 1969), 72.

67. Ibid., 73.
68. André Parrot, *The Temple of Jerusalem,* trans. B. E. Hooke (London: SCM Press, Ltd., 1957), 96.
69. Shibayama, 235.
70. Ibid., 238.
71. Dogen, *A Primer of Soto Zen,* 27.
72. Suzuki, *Manual of Zen Buddhism,* 133.
73. "Ikkyu's Skeletons," *The Buddha Eye,* 79.
74. Shinran, Gotaku Shaku, *Tannisho: A Shin Buddhist Classic,* trans. Taitetsu Unno (Honolulu: Buddhist Study Center Press, 1984), 8.
75. Ibid.
76. Hans Fischer-Barnicol, "Fragen aus Fernost. Eine Begegnung mit dem japanischen Philosophen Nishitani," *Hochland* 58 (1966): 210; cited by Hans Waldenfels, *Absolute Nothingness: Foundations for a Buddhist–Christian Dialogue,* trans. J. W. Heisig (New York: Paulist Press, 1980), 157.
77. Shibayama, 100.
78. Ibid., 101.
79. Suzuki, "What Is the 'I'?", *The Buddha Eye,* 34.
80. Dumoulin, 1:191.
81. David J. and Indrani Kalupahana, *The Way of Siddhartha: A Life of the Buddha* (Boulder, CO: Shambala, 1982), 70–71.
82. Ibid., 72.
83. Quoted by R. H. Blyth, *Zen and Zen Classics,* ed. Frederick Franck (New York: Vintage Books, 1978), 218.
84. Tanabe, xxxv.
85. Ibid., 9
86. Ibid., lv.
87. Ibid., 27.
88. *The Threefold Lotus Sutra: Innumerable Meanings, The Lotus Flower of the Wonderful Law, and Meditation on the Bodhisattva Universal Virtue,* trans. Bunno Kato et al. (Tokyo: Kosei Publishing Co., 1975), 112.
89. Ibid., 114.
90. *Saddharmapundarika,* 4:101ff; in *The Buddhist Tradition in India, China and Japan,* 89.
91. Ibid., 90.
92. *The Threefold Lotus Sutra,* 115.
93. *The Buddhist Tradition in India, China and Japan,* 87.

94. Dogen, *Primer,* 42.

95. From Siksasamuccaya, 257; in *The Buddhist Tradition in India, China and Japan,* 101.

96. Suzuki, *Manual of Zen Buddhism,* 129.

97. Shibayama, 42.

98. Ibid., 43.

99. Suzuki, "What Is the 'I'?", *The Buddha Eye,* 33–34.

100. Ibid., 34.

101. John Daido Loori, *Mountain Record of Zen Talks,* ed. Bonnie Myotai Treace (Boston: Shambala, 1988), 77.

102. Shibayama, 27.

103. Ibid., 28.

104. Ibid., 9.

105. Thomas Merton, *Zen and the Birds of Appetite.* New York: New Directions Books, 1968), 54.

106. Shibayama, 25.

107. Daisetz Teitaro Suzuki, "Self the Unattainable," *The Buddha Eye,* 21.

108. Masao Abe, "God, Emptiness, and the True Self," *The Buddha Eye,* 70.

109. Quoted by Shibayama, 111.

110. Ibid., 110.

111. *Buddha-karita of Asvaghosha,* 160.

112. Ibid., 84.

113. Daisetz Teitaro Suzuki, *Outlines of Mahayana Buddhism* (London: Luzac and Company, 1907; reprint, New York: Schocken Books, 1963), 282.

114. *Zen Poems of China and Japan,* 52.

115. *The Threefold Lotus Sutra,* 209, 210.

116. Ibid., 209.

117. Dogen, *Shobogenzo,* "Keisei-sanshoku," quoted by Kim, 205.

118. Robert Buchanan, "The Ballad of Judas Iscariot," *The Standard Book of British and American Verse* (Garden City, NY: Garden City Publishing Company, Inc., 1932), 611ff; quoted by Morton T. Kelsey, *The Other Side of Silence: A Guide to Christian Meditation* (New York: Paulist Press, 1976), 279.

119. Quoted by Taitetsu Unno, "Afterword," to Shinran, *Tannisho,* 46.

120. *Zen Poems of China and Japan,* 5.

121. Pseudo-Dionysius, *The Divine Names,* 1:2, trans. Colm Luibheid, in *Pseudo-Dionysius: The Complete Works* (New York: Paulist Press, 1987), 50.

122. Ibid.

123. Pseudo-Dionysius, *The Mystical Theology,* 1:3; in *Complete Works,* 137.

124. Suzuki, *Essays in Zen Buddhism,* 265.

125. *Zen Poems of China and Japan,* 7.

126. Suzuki, *Essays in Zen Buddhism,* 245.

127. Sosan, "On Believing in Mind," in Suzuki, *Manual of Zen Buddhism,* 82.

List of References

Athanasius. *On the Incarnation*. Trans. Penelope Lawson. New York: Macmillan Publishing Company, 1946.

Augustine. *Confessions*. Trans. R. S. Pine-Coffin. Harmondsworth, England: Penguin Books, 1961.

Augustine. *The Spirit and the Letter*. In *Augustine: Later Works*. Trans. John Burnaby. Philadelphia: Westminster Press, 1955.

Bloom, Alfred. *Shinran's Gospel of Pure Grace*. Monographs of the Association for Asian Studies, No. 20. Tucson, AZ: University of Arizona Press, 1965.

Blyth, R. H. *Zen and Zen Classics*. Ed. Frederick Franck. New York: Vintage Books, 1978.

Buchanan, Robert. "The Ballad of Judas Iscariot." In *The Standard Book of British and American Verse*. Garden City, NY: Garden City Publishing Company, Inc., 1932.

Chang, Garma C. C. *The Buddhist Teaching of Totality: The Philosophy of Hwa Yen Buddhism*. University Park, PA: Pennsylvania State University Press, 1986.

Conze, Edward. *Buddhist Scriptures*. Harmondsworth, England: Penguin Books, 1959.

Cook, Francis H. *Hua-yen Buddhism: The Jewel Net of Indra*. University Park, PA: Pennsylvania State University Press, 1977.

Cowell, E. B., et al., eds. and trans. *Buddhist Mahayana Texts.* The Sacred Books of the East, vol. 49; ed. F. Max Müller. Oxford: Clarendon Press, 1894. Reprint, New York: Dover Publications, Inc., 1969.

De Bary, William Theodore, ed. *The Buddhist Tradition in India, China and Japan.* New York: Vintage Books, 1972.

Dogen. "Dogen's Bendowa." Trans. Norman Waddell and Masao Abe. *The Eastern Buddhist* 4 (1971): 124–57.

Dogen. *A Primer of Soto Zen: A Translation of Dogen's Shobogenzo Zuimonki.* Trans. Reiho Masanuga. An East-West Center Book. Honolulu: University of Hawaii Press, 1985.

Dogen. *Moon in a Dewdrop: Writings of Zen Master Dogen.* Ed. Kazuaki Tanashi. Trans. Robert Aitken et al. San Francisco: North Point Press, 1985.

Dumoulin, Heinrich. *Zen Buddhism: A History.* Vol. 1, *India and China.* Trans. James W. Heisig and Paul Knitter. New York: Macmillan Publishing Company, 1988.

Fox, Douglas A. *The Heart of Buddhist Wisdom: A Translation of the Heart Sutra With Historical Introduction and Commentary.* Studies in Asian Thought and Religion, Vol. 3. Lewiston, NY: Edwin Mellen Press, 1985.

Franck, Frederick, ed. *The Buddha Eye: An Anthology of the Kyoto School.* New York: Crossroad, 1982.

Hakeda, Yoshito S. *Kukai: Major Works, Translated, with an Account of His Life and a Study of His Thought.* New York: Columbia University Press, 1972.

Kalupahana, David J. and Indrani. *The Way of Siddhartha: A Life of the Buddha.* Boulder, CO: Shambala, 1982.

Jeremias, Joachim. *The Parables of Jesus.* Revised ed. Trans. S. H. Hooke. New York: Charles Scribner's Sons, 1963.

Kato, Bunno et al., trans. *The Threefold Lotus Sutra: Innumerable Meanings, The Lotus Flower of the Wonderful Law, and Meditation on the Boddhisattva Universal Virtue.* Tokyo: Kosei Publishing Co., 1975.

Kim, Hee-Jin. *Dogen Kigen: Mystical Realist.* Revised ed. Tucson, AZ: University of Arizona Press, 1987.

Loori, John Daido. "The Miracle of Aliveness." *Mountain Record* 7, no. 1 (1988): 2–9.

Loori, John Daido. *Mountain Record of Zen Talks.* Ed. Bonnie Myotai Treace. Boston: Shambala, 1988.

Loori, John Daido. "Zazen: The Still Point." *Mountain Record* 6, no. 3 (1987): 4–10.

Merton, Thomas. *Zen and the Birds of Appetite.* New York: New Directions Books, 1968.

Nicholas of Cusa. *On God as Not-other.* A Translation and an Appraisal of *De Li Non Aliud.* Trans. Jasper Hopkins. Minneapolis: University of Minnesota Press, 1979.

The Nishi Hongwanji Commission on the Promotion of Religious Education. *Shinran in the Contemporary World.* Second ed. Kyoto, Japan: Hongwanji International Center, 1979.

Parrot, André. *The Temple of Jerusalem.* Trans. B. E. Hooke. London: SCM Press, Ltd., 1957.

Pieris, Aloysius. *Love Meets Wisdom: A Christian Experience of Buddhism.* Maryknoll, NY: Orbis Books, 1988.

Pseudo-Dionysius. *The Complete Works.* Trans. Colm Luibheid. New York: Paulist Press, 1987.

Pye, Michael. *Skilful Means: A Concept in Mahayana Buddhism.* London: Duckworth, 1978.

Ricoeur, Paul. "Beyond Autonomy and Heteronomy." Lecture at the University of Chicago, 1987.

Shibayama, Zenkei. *Zen Comments on the Mumonkan.* Trans. Sumiko Kudo. San Francisco: Harper & Row, 1984.

Shinran, Gutoku Shaku. *The Kyogyoshinsho: The Collection of Passages Expounding the True Teaching, Living, Faith, and Realizing of the Pure Land.* Ed. Eastern Buddhist Society. Trans. Daisetz Teitaro Suzuki. Kyoto: Shinshu Otaniha, 1973.

Shinran, Gutoku Shaku. *Tannisho: A Shin Buddhist Classic.* Trans. Taitetsu Unno. Honolulu: Buddhist Study Center Press, 1984.

Smith, Wilfred Cantwell. *Towards a World Theology: Faith and the Comparative History of Religions.* Philadelphia: Westminster Press, 1981.

Stryk, Lucien et al., trans. *Zen Poems of China and Japan: The Crane's Bill*. Garden City, NY: Anchor Books, 1973.

Suzuki, Daisetz Teitaro. *An Introduction to Zen Buddhism*. New York: Grove Press, Inc., 1964.

Suzuki, Daisetz Teitaro. *Essays in Zen Buddhism. First Series.* New York: Grove Press, Inc., 1949, 1985.

Suzuki, Daisetz Teitaro. *Manual of Zen Buddhism*. New York: Grove Press, Inc., 1960.

Suzuki, Daisetz Teitaro. *Outlines of Mahayana Buddhism*. London: Luzac and Company, 1907. Reprint, New York: Schocken Books, 1967.

Takeuchi, Yoshinori. *The Heart of Buddhism: In Search of the Timeless Spirit of Primitive Buddhism*. Ed. and trans. James W. Heisig. New York: Crossroad, 1983.

Tanabe, Hajime. *Philosophy as Metanoetics*. Trans. Yoshinori Takeuchi et al. Berkeley: University of California Press, 1986.

Toynbee, Arnold. *Christianity among the Religions of the World*. New York: Charles Scribner's Sons, 1957.

Vatican II. *Nostra Aetate (Declaration on the Relation of the Church to Non-Christian Religions), in Vatican Council II: The Conciliar and Post Conciliar Documents*. Ed. Austin Flannery. Collegeville, MN: Liturgical Press, 1984.

Waldenfels, Hans. *Absolute Nothingness: Foundations for a Buddhist-Christian Dialogue*. Trans. J. W. Heisig. New York: Paulist Press, 1980.